What Economists Should Do

What Economists Should Do

In Defense of Mainstream Economic Thought

David G. Tuerck

BEP

BUSINESS EXPERT PRESS

Leader in applied, concise business books

What Economists Should Do: In Defense of Mainstream Economic Thought

Copyright © Business Expert Press, LLC, 2022.

Cover design by Charlene Kronstedt

Interior design by Exeter Premedia Services Private Ltd., Chennai, India

First published in 2022 by
Business Expert Press, LLC
222 East 46th Street, New York, NY 10017
www.businessexpertpress.com

ISBN-13: 978-1-63742-232-8 (paperback)
ISBN-13: 978-1-63742-233-5 (e-book)

Business Expert Press Economics and Public Policy Collection

First edition: 2022

10 9 8 7 6 5 4 3 2 1

I would like to dedicate this book to Prema,
who inspires me in all I do.

Description

The discipline of economics suffers from a great deal of dissention among its practitioners. There are a number of economic fields that challenge the validity of "neoclassical economics" or what can be called "mainstream economics." The neoclassical school, which emerged in the 1870s, advanced the study of economics by developing a theory of value based on utility. The earlier classical school saw value as based on the labor content of goods. Neoclassical economics is what college students are taught in their courses on microeconomics. Instruction in microeconomics is centered on the principle that, for any good, price will adjust until supply equals demand.

Challenges to this principle come from several sources: behavioral economics, neuroeconomics, Austrian economics, Keynesian economics, and others. A common thread running through these fields is that neoclassical economics rests on unrealistic assumptions and must therefore be questioned for its usefulness.

This book argues that, contrary to the critics, neoclassical economics is the only method available to economists for bringing about rational economic policy choices. Irrational policy choices are the result of voters and politicians letting sentiments, as Adam Smith defined them, get in the way of rational thought. Neoclassical economics predicts that minimum wage laws will cause unemployment of low-wage workers. Yet minimum wage laws remain popular with both voters and politicians. It is the job of economists to question this popularity.

It is not enough, however, for economists to provide accurate predictions. They must also goad voters and politicians into seeing the irrationality of adopting harmful policy measures such as minimum wage laws, buy-American rules, and corporate tax increases. Economists therefore must play a role akin to preachers, in that their effectiveness depends not just on their analytical work, but also on their success in instilling rational thought into their audience.

Keywords

mainstream economics; neoclassical economics; classical economics; marginal utility; perfect competition; behavioral economics; prospect theory; hyperbolic discounting; exponential discounting; Keynesian economics; folk economics; moral sentiments; comparative advantage; Austrian economics; catallactics; Turing machine; rational choice; cognitive science; neuroeconomics; cost–benefit analysis; project labor agreements; prevailing wage law; modern monetary theory; usury; government infrastructure; marginal propensity to consume; gross domestic product; memes; mercantilism; functionalism; eliminativism; scaffolding; intentionality; computable general equilibrium model; real cost; opportunity cost

Contents

Preface

Economists seldom ask themselves whether they do anything useful or not. Probably, economists as a species consider it unnecessary to engage in such self-reflection. After all, there seems to be a robust market for people to teach economics or provide economic advice. The American Economic Association claims 21,000 plus members. A U.S. Department of Labor report indicates that 17,520 economists were employed in the United States in May 2020 and earned an average annual wage of $120,880. Almost any graduate student in economics can expect to find a good job upon completing his PhD.

Yet, there is much turmoil within the ranks of people who call themselves economists. For one thing, economists notoriously disagree about the substance of their research. An old joke goes, "If all the economists were laid end to end, they would never reach a conclusion." If economists themselves are in constant disagreement, how can the opinions of any of them be trusted? Then there is also a wide-ranging criticism of the validity of what is labeled here as "mainstream economics."

Disclosure: Over the last several years, I have directed efforts to build large-scale computer models of the economy—just the sort of endeavor that some modern critics eschew. I see the construction of such models as needed for addressing one of the most important issues of our time, which is to say how tax law changes affect the economy.

Yes, I have my own beliefs. I believe that increases in the corporate tax rate will have negative effects on jobs and wages. But I have to defend my beliefs in terms of the robustness of my models, not any blind faith in the rightness of my views. And debating such matters is what economists should, in fact, do. That, at least, produces a hope that competing models will become more robust and thus more useful in framing policy. What economists must do is work to make their models increasingly descriptive of the functioning of the economy.

This point of view is at odds with the Virginia school of political economy, on which I was nurtured back in the 1960s. The Virginia school rejects the view that politicians should be seen primarily as attempting to further the public interest. It is necessary to study politicians as people who act in their self-interest. While I certainly accept that view, I do not share the Virginia school's disdain for mathematical modeling as a key element in the economist's job description.

This book appears during a particularly tumultuous episode in U.S. economic history. For the two-year period leading up to its publication, there appears to have been an abandonment of the whole discipline of economics in enacting policies aimed at offsetting the economic effects of the COVID-19 pandemic and in running massive federal deficits.

John Maynard Keynes, on whom we will focus later, famously said that

> practical men who believe themselves to be quite exempt from any intellectual influence, are usually the slaves of some defunct economist. Madmen in authority, who hear voices in the air, are distilling their frenzy from some academic scribbler of a few years back (Keynes 1936, 383).

I think that Keynes had it backwards (and, ironically, could have been talking about himself). It is economists who believe themselves to be exempt from any limitation or what we will call "sentiments" and who have become the slaves of practical men. It is my hope that this book will offer some ideas to my fellow economists for finding our way out of this servitude.

My further hope is that this book will help galvanize the noneconomists among my readers to see two facts: (1) that they are being manipulated by politicians into settling for policies that run counter to their interests, and (2) that they will be able to protect their interests only by injecting rationality into choices from which it is conspicuously absent. Finally, I hope to goad my fellow economists out of the practice of talking mostly among themselves and largely about matters of little value to anyone but themselves, and into the practice of making their discipline useful, for a change, to the public they serve.

Numerous fields of study operate under the rubric of economics while attempting to show the obsolescence of what we can call "mainstream economics." This book identifies some of the most prominent of these fields of study as it attempts to show the legitimacy and importance of the very same mainstream economics.

Ironically, perhaps, half of the standard two-semester micro/macro sequence in introductory college economics is devoted to mainstream economics. The "micro" half of that sequence is almost entirely mainstream, as I shall define it here. (Think about the study of supply and demand.) The micro/macro sequence is followed through the graduate curriculum and to the top PhD courses.

The whole idea that there exists a mainstream economics on which its critics feed brings to mind the ancient Greek myth of the ouroboros, which was a dragon that ate its own tail. That's because there exists a kind of synergy between the mainstream practitioners and their critics, all feeding on each other's claims to intellectual pre-eminence. That process does nothing to make economics effective for bringing about rational policy choices. My goal here is to slay the ouroboros dragon.

Acknowledgments

My thanks to my wife, Prema Popat, and my Beacon Hill Institute colleague, Frank Conte, for reading and critiquing the manuscript. Their help made all the difference in what finally showed up in print. I also wish to thank Scott Eisenberg for his support and patience throughout the project.

CHAPTER 1

Introduction

Economics, as a discipline, suffers from internecine strife—competing schools of thought that have in common only one feature—a hostility to what we can call "mainstream economics." Why this strife? The answer lies in part with what one writer has branded "folk economics." This is the economics that has a grip on people's thinking and that impedes any progress economists can make in improving public policy outcomes.

Paul Rubin defines folk economics as "the economic notions that naive (untrained) individuals have and the perceptions of such individuals about the economy" (Rubin 2003, 157). Folk economics derives from the "zero-sum" hypothesis, whereby one person's economic gain is necessarily another person's loss. Thus, any gains from free trade bring about losses by people (often workers) who don't benefit from it. Thus, also, as in Marxian thinking, surplus value generated by labor goes to the capitalist and not the worker.

To look more deeply, consider politicians who simultaneously condemn trade deficits and extol capital inflows from foreign countries, not realizing that capital inflows are just the mirror image of trade deficits. You can't have one without the other. Consider also politicians who simultaneously condemn corporate tax cuts and complain about globalized capital markets, not realizing that the benefits of such tax cuts in a globalized economy mostly flow to workers and not capitalists. Consider the political support of a $15 minimum wage combined with evidence of the millions of jobs that would be lost by the imposition of a wage that high. These are all examples of folk economics—views, however erroneous, that plant themselves in people's mind and are next to impossible to root out.

Robbins' Definition of Economics

What then are economists supposed to do? In 1932, Lionel Robbins gave us the most often used answer: "Economics," he said, "is the science which studies human behavior as a relationship between ends and scarce means which have alternative uses" (Robbins 1932, 16). It might be said that Robbins' definition is at the heart of mainstream economics.

Robbins assumed that people are rational optimizers. When the consumer walks into a store, he chooses among all the different combinations of goods available to him in such a way as to maximize utility. To maximize utility is to choose the combination of goods that the shopper most prefers and also can afford. This was worked out as a mathematical exercise by William Stanley Jevons (Jevons 1871) in the 1870s.

Even though Robbins' definition appears in almost every introductory textbook, there are important schools of thought, within economics, that argue strongly against its use. Indeed, it often seems that Robbins' definition has gone out of style. Years of research in the fields of behavioral economics and neuroeconomics have created doubts that actual economic choices work as defined by Robbins. There is no maximizing going on, say these critics. Arguments from cognitive science claim that there is no decision maker who makes the choices said to be made by the prototype shopper in the store. It seems that the entire first-semester course in economics proceeds on a false premise and should be thrown out in favor of a more "realistic" approach to the subject—although we will see that one of the most prominent proponents of behavioral economics suggests otherwise.

Gruber's Gaffe

Meanwhile, some economists seem eager to make themselves—and their profession—appear ridiculous. In 2013, Jonathan Gruber, an economics professor at MIT and an architect of the Obama-era Affordable Healthcare Act, went on a panel to declare that certain portions of the Act were written in a deliberately misleading fashion in order to compensate for "the stupidity of the American voter," who would have opposed the Act had it been written in a more transparent fashion.[1] Gruber's choice of words brought him widespread condemnation.

Gruber deserves this condemnation but not because he insulted the American voter. He deserves it because he failed to realize that his sole job as an economist was to make sure that voters understood exactly how an Act that he coauthored and supported would affect them. As an economist, he had no business, trying to keep voters misinformed so that they would go along with a piece of legislation that he was paid to create.

There is, in fact, plenty of opportunity for politicians, with the help of their economic advisors, to misinform the public. Behavioral economics has found that people base their policy choices on how issues are framed, making them vulnerable to manipulation by politicians (and sometimes by economists) with a policy axe to grind. Neuroeconomics has found that people do not think in terms of all the choices available to them but only the choices with which they are immediately familiar.

Despite these criticisms, practitioners of mainstream economics, as defined by Robbins, continue to assume that people are rational in their economic choices. This book will argue that it is precisely the fact that mainstream economics assumes rational choice—despite the critics—that makes it the only tool for correcting the muddle left by folk economics and propagated by politicians posing as economists.

Mainstream economic thinking lives on through the "neoclassical school" of economics, which emerged in the 1870s and reached maturity in the 1920s. This school became so named mainly because it debunked the labor theory of value, prominent in the writings of Smith and Ricardo, who, along with J.B. Say, were the most prominent of the "classical" economists.

Some prestigious economists, notably A.K. Sen, reject the idea that people are rational optimizers. Such people, if they exist, are "rational fools," says Sen (Sen 1977, 317). I will not argue with Sen. I will recognize, specifically, that people are as motivated by "sentiment" as they are by logic. But in my formulation, people also act in their own interest, as they see it, motivated, we hope, by efforts by economists to induce them to choose rationally.

---

[1] See https://www.youtube.com/watch?v=G790p0LcgbI.

The Role of Rational Choice

This book makes a simple argument: If we are going to study economics, we need to understand the role of rational choice in the performance of the economy. Rational choice enters at three levels: (1) the level at which people make economic choices, (2) the level at which they theorize about how people make economic choices, and (3) the level at which they make choices about economic policies that affect their economic choices. At the first level, the question is whether the individual decision maker (or "economic agent") follows certain rules for rational choice in making economic choices. At the second level, the question is whether to assume that people follow the same rules when we theorize about economic choices. At the third level, the question is whether people make rational policy choices.

So, for example, at the first level, there are rules for rational choice when a shopper enters a hardware store and must choose between the goods on the shelves. How does he make the selection that maximizes utility? Or how does a business make investment decisions that maximize profits? Then, at the next level, if an issue over, say, tax policy arises, the question is whether people affected by that issue think rationally about it. Suppose that the government considers the imposition of a sales tax, and we want to know how the tax will affect the prices of goods in the hardware store and also how customers react to the change in those prices. Do we assume that the store owner and his customers will think rationally in our efforts to answer these questions? Will the price of hardware rise? Will customers buy fewer power drills if their price rises? Finally, at the third level, do we choose rationally in imposing a sales tax? Would a sales tax be superior or inferior to an income tax for raising government revenue?

While economists address all three levels, this book is primarily concerned with level (3): It considers how economists can advise on economic policies, given a predisposition by the general public to think irrationally about those issues. The reader might well be shocked by the implication that economists should concern themselves with the obstacles to good policies presented by the predisposition on the part of the public to choose irrationally. It sounds like I am urging economists to preach against irrationality in policy making. Well, actually, I am. Some will view this as a form of economic apostasy.

CHAPTER 2

Preaching Economics

In a lecture entitled "The Economist as Preacher," delivered in 1980, the late George Stigler warned economists against preaching. To illustrate the sort of preaching that economists should avoid, Stigler cited a passage from the *Wealth of Nations* (widely regarded as a foundational contribution to economics), in which Adam Smith condemned the "debasement of currency." Stigler quoted Smith as saying,

> By means of those operations the princes and sovereign states which performed them were enabled, in appearance, to pay their debts and to fulfill their engagements with a smaller quantity of silver than would otherwise have been requisite. It was indeed in appearance only; for their creditors were really defrauded of a part of what was due to them (Stigler 1982, 4).

Stigler sympathized with Smith's argument. But he didn't like Smith's use of the word "defrauded." By using that word, said Stigler, Smith lapsed into preaching.

Stigler used his lecture to express his disapproval of economists like Smith who preached. "The great economists," he said, "have not been preoccupied with preaching" (Stigler 1982, 5). (One must suspect that, by this criterion, there were precious few great economists.)

Continuing in his lecture, Stigler allowed that while he could sympathize with Smith's criticisms of the "private behavior" of individuals, such criticisms were, in principle, "not defensible." What was defensible? Stigler's answer was that:

> social policies and institutions, not individual behavior, are the proper object of the economist-preacher's solicitude. This orientation is demanded by the very logic of economic theory: we

deal with people who maximize their utility, and it would be both inconsistent and idle for us to urge people not to do so (Stigler 1982, 6).

Stigler did not stop there. As he continued, he condemned the very criticism of "social policies and institutions" of which he had, in just a few words earlier, approved. This he did by turning the goal of efficiency into a bugbear and by condemning its pursuit by policy advisors.

"Efficiency," he said, has become the mantra of economists, *qua* policy advisors. Economists had convinced themselves that they could legitimately criticize policies that were demonstrably at odds with the goals of society and do so without taking a position one way or another on the ethical legitimacy of those goals. This, he said, was a mistaken idea.

Stigler asked rhetorically how "the economist can operate so extensively as the critic of policy when he is not in possession of a persuasive ethical system" (Stigler 1982, 8). How does the economist justify his preaching when he has explicitly claimed to be neutral on the matter of ethics? The economist, Stigler said, would defend himself by arguing:

> that he needs no ethical system to criticize error: he is simply a well-trained political arithmetician. He lives in a world of social *mistakes*, ancient and modern, subtle and simple, and since he is simply pointing out to society that what it seeks, it is seeking inefficiently, he need not quarrel with what it seeks.
>
> A world full of mistakes, and capable of producing new mistakes quite as rapidly as the economists can correct the old mistakes! Such well-meaning, incompetent societies need their economic efficiency experts, and we are their self-chosen saviors (Stigler 1982, 8).

Thus, in Stigler's view, economists who tried to offer policy advice were fooling themselves if they thought that they could do so on ethically neutral grounds. And because they could not, they were obligated, as scientists, to forgo offering policy advice—or so he implied. The idea of an ethics-free advisor, Stigler said, "is profoundly mistaken." One reason is that there have been "vigorous controversies over the goals of policy" throughout history.

Now, says Stigler, there has been enough debate over the goals of society. The goals are well settled. A second and more important reason is the contradiction inherent to assuming, on the one hand, that people are utility maximizers and then, on the other, that "the political activity of men bears little relationship to their desires" (Stigler 1982, 9).

A theory of persistent political mistakes, he says, "has little to commend it." Going on, he says:

> To believe, year after year, decade after decade, that the protective tariffs or usury laws to be found in most lands are due to confusion rather than purposeful action is singularly obfuscatory. Mistakes are indeed made by the best of men and the best of nations, but after a century are we not entitled to question whether the so-called "mistakes" produce only unintended results (Stigler 1982, 10)?

Waxing philosophical, Stigler pointed out that "a theory that says a large set of persistent policies are mistaken is profoundly anti-intellectual unless it is joined to a theory of mistakes." Economists prone to preaching have to recognize that the persistence of seemingly inefficient policies suggests that those policies are "tolerably efficient," after all (Stigler 1982, 10).

Thus, Stigler tells economists that they should provide a theory of mistakes before they start finding mistakes in people's choices of social policies and institutions. There is irony here: Stigler accused his fellow economists of mistakenly finding mistakes in social policy without providing a theory of how these economists identify mistakes. Where was the theory of mistakes by which he made this accusation?

Many who have followed Stigler's career and writings would find his admonitions against preaching to be hypocritical in the extreme. In *Chicago Fundamentalism*, Craig F. Freedman correctly states that "Stigler was a closet moralist, acting in much the same way as he conceptualized the motives and objectives of his early predecessors." About this, Freedman opined that "morality … can permeate analysis in a less than desirable fashion if transformed into ideological imperatives," which, Freedman argues, left Stigler "with a distinct blind spot" (Freedman 2008, 27).

Contrary to his own advice, Stigler was indeed a preacher but in precisely the way an economist should be. He preached as he should have by adhering to the rational choice model, which, I shall argue, is the one weapon in the economics arsenal that can be used to good effect in arguing public policy issues. So, if Stigler was a closet moralist, one can only say that it's too bad he didn't come out of the closet.

Taken at his word in this lecture, Stigler would strip economics of any value for improving economic outcomes. If a policy—even a bad policy—has been around long enough, then there is no criticizing it because it must, by reason of its longevity, be a good policy. Fortunately, the actual Stigler did not allow this kind of illogic to get in the way of his sermonizing.

Wittman's Argument

In his 1995 book, *The Myth of Democratic Failure*, Donald Wittman reinforces Stigler's view that policy making (at least policy making in democratic societies) performs with "tolerable efficiency." He sets out to show "that democratic markets are organized to promote wealth-maximizing outcomes, that these markets are highly competitive, and that political and bureaucratic entrepreneurs are rewarded for efficient behavior." Whereas critics of democracy claim that markets and only markets can be made to work well, Wittman argues that "both political and economic markets work well" (Wittman 1995, 2).

Wittman's self-appointed task is to "cure the schizophrenia facing most economists, who believe that economic markets work well, but political markets work poorly." Wittman feels that he does not have to correct only for his fellow economists' schizophrenia. There is also the need to correct the "blindness of many sociologists" when it comes to understanding "rational behavior and competition" and the need to help political scientists "develop a consistent theoretical approach" (Wittman 1995, 2).

A tall order, indeed. Yet, Wittman is able to congratulate himself for rising to the challenge. In a manner reminiscent of John Stuart Mill's pronouncement of 1848 that "in the laws of value" nothing remained "to clear up," Wittman tells us that, with his book, "the burden of proof will be on those who argue that democratic political markets are inefficient" (Wittman 1995, 2).

As I write now, in 2021, it seems that recent events have lessened this burden substantially. The idea that U.S. economic policies are, in Wittman's words, "not too inefficient" (Wittman 1995, 184) would command far less agreement today than it might have when Stigler preached against preaching (1980) and when Wittman published his book (1995). The current political climate is, by my observation, the most rancorous of the last 60 years. Political control swings from one party to another, seemingly with no rhyme or reason. Federal spending policies have gone off the rails.

The deeper question for Stigler and Wittman is what economists are supposed to do if they recognize political markets as efficient. If there are few inefficiencies to expose, there is little to do but recognize that those that remain are acceptable, simply because they have survived politically

Meanwhile, Stigler's insistence that "individual economic actors maximize utility" is under a growing assault. The assault comes from various schools of thought, principally among them behavioral economics, Austrian economics, Keynesian economics, cognitive economics, and neuroeconomics.

In one way or another, these schools reject the view that there exist utility-maximizing economic agents who are "whole persons" and who buy and sell goods at market-determined prices. The rational choice model assumes that it is the job of economists to predict the choices made by exactly such persons. George Stigler was a thoroughgoing defender of that idea.

What This Book Argues

This book argues (1) that the assault on rational choice threatens to reduce economics to irrelevance and (2) that economists can be rescued from this irrelevance only if they become willing to embrace the very "preacher" role that Stigler condemned. In making this argument I will stipulate, in accord with the critics of the rational choice model, that people have a predisposition to think irrationally when it comes to economic issues. Irrationality is the original sin of economic decision making. Given this predisposition, the job of economists is to encourage people to think rationally instead. To do so, economists need to understand that, while not on a mission from God (with apologies to the Blues Brothers), they are on a mission of the highest humanitarian calling. The assault on rational choice is as old as sin and as deadly for its effects on man's lives and souls.

The dissenting schools of thought differ in many important ways, but running through them is a common theme—that economic agents, defined as "whole selves," do not maximize utility. People act in their self-interest but do not maximize. Or they do not act in their self-interest at all. Or it is not "whole selves" that act self-interestedly but rather the "homonuclei" of which selves are composed. Or people might at some level want to maximize utility but are prevented from doing so because of how their brains are wired.

It would seem that the lay observer might regard these assertions with a certain amount of amusement—economists giving up on their hopeless quest to agree on what they believe. When he gave his lecture, Stigler could probably sense what was already afoot in terms of the deconstruction of economics. Were he alive today, he would recoil in horror over the subsequent attack on the rational choice model.

I submit that neither economists nor lay people can dismiss the growing empirical and philosophical corpus of thought that challenges the rational choice model. Indeed, I think that there is one lesson of the dissenting schools—that a "status quo" bias militates against rational choice—that defenders of the rational choice model must accept and incorporate into their work as preachers (or, more exactly, the kind of preachers I urge them to become). If people suffer a status quo bias and if that undermines rational choice, then the economist must take on the task of challenging that bias.

In my judgment, there is but one role that the economist can play in leading his audience out of the wilderness and that is to show them what rational thought looks like. This is not just for pedagogical purposes. First, people are at some level constrained to act rationally by the marketplace: Failure to act rationally carries penalties, and willingness to do so carries rewards. It is well for people to know and act upon the principles of rational choice in their everyday economic choices. Second, people care about how they are perceived by other people and are reluctant to be shown as thinking irrationally when they appeal to other people for their cooperation around political issues. Third, people are willing to abandon demonstrably inconsistent thinking when it is pointed out to them.

Ricardo on Wine and Cloth

Consider David Ricardo's demonstration of comparative advantage, which led to the repeal of the British Corn Laws in 1846. Using his example, suppose that England and Portugal both produce wine and cloth, even though England has a comparative advantage in cloth and Portugal has a comparative advantage in wine. The Portuguese insist on producing their own cloth on the theory that it costs less, in terms of labor hours, to produce cloth in Portugal than it does in England. Suppose, however, that both countries confer with an economist, who explains that both could have more cloth and more wine if Portugal exported wine to England and England exported cloth to Portugal. In this fashion, the economist deploys the rational choice model to correct for a flaw in trade policy that reduces the amount of wine and cloth available to both countries.

It is important to recognize the preacher-like role that the economist plays in this scenario. To improve the well-being of the English and the Portuguese, he has to convince both countries to shift production out of the product in which it has a comparative disadvantage and into the product in which it has a comparative advantage. To do this, he deploys a model in which it is consumption, not production, that matters to both countries—and this contrary to the fact that it is production that the trade authorities want to put first. He deploys a model based on rational choice when actual choice has been irrational.

Because utility comes from the consumption of cloth and wine, the English maximize utility by shifting labor from the production of wine and to cloth, and the Portuguese do so by shifting production from cloth to wine. The preaching comes in when economists insist on maximizing consumption and therefore utility rather than production. The goal of economics is not to protect producers in their chosen occupation but to maximize utility. As Adam Smith put it, "Consumption is the sole end and purpose of all production."

One of the mistakes that rational choice dissidents make is to ignore the distinction between rational choice itself and the context that is necessary for choices to be made rationally. Teenagers parked in a car on warm summer evening or a couple of shopaholics who stroll by Tiffany's after they have hit the lottery are not putting themselves in a context that encourages rational choice. There is a clear difference between what rational choice for these individuals would look like and what they choose in a context that makes rational choice unlikely.

Economists who operate in the rational choice tradition build models in which economic agents choose rationally and then employ those models to analyze policy questions. So, for example, David Ricardo's comparative advantage model assumed rational thinking of precisely the kind that was absent from the British trade policy of his day, with the country protecting its agricultural sector from competition from imports. Ricardo's model had a cognitive purpose, which was to cause people to eliminate inconsistencies in their thinking that prevented them from having as much cloth and wine as they could have, given known differences in comparative costs.

The construction of a model may or may not induce the policy makers to whom it is presented to make rational choices. Portuguese cloth producers may not wish to lose business to their English competitors and might pressure the Portuguese government to prevent the importation of English cloth. What then does the economist do? One answer is that, having done his job, the economist must step aside and let the policy makers decide. Another answer is that the economist's job is not merely to build a model that would be useful to policy makers but also to confront policy makers with the consequences of irrational choice, for example, less cloth (or wine) to consume. The economist's responsibility is to consumers, not producers. The economist cannot force policy makers to open up trade, but he can goad them into confronting whatever values drive them to put the interests of producers ahead of consumers.

I argue that Stigler's admonitions against preaching are off the mark and that Wittman is naïve in his optimistic assessment of the performance of political markets. It would be an exercise in malpractice for a building contractor to permit his client to forge ahead with a plan that is doomed to fail. It would be an act of malpractice for the economist to condone Portuguese policy makers' exclusion of English cloth on the basis of a spurious argument that they were doing so in the name of the public interest.

The problem for economists is that policy makers, that is to say, politicians, occupy a universe in which there is little accountability for mistakes and in which there are rewards for camouflaging the truth. Thus, the economist must decide whether his job ends with a presentation of the facts or only when he has done all he can to make voters and politicians own up to the facts, as presented. The latter requires preaching.

I argue that economists have a duty to goad voters and politicians into thinking rationally. Economists should be preachers in exactly the sense that Stigler condemned, in that they should reveal where social policies suffer from remedial internal inconsistencies. In this book, I lay out my recommendations for just how the economist-preacher should write his sermons. I plunge further into this uncharted territory by describing the ethical system from which the economist-preacher derives his authority to preach.

I use the word "goad" advisedly. The preacher's constituency is his congregation and the economist's constituency is the voting public. Like preachers, at least since the witch trials, economists cannot compel their constituents to pay heed to their sermons. But, like preachers, economists can legitimately use the instruments and rhetorical devices at their disposal to induce rational choice.

Anyone who has witnessed the expansion in the federal government over the first half of 2021 would justifiably suspect that systematic errors are taking place. It is simply not realistic to see the political process as successfully channeling voters' preferences into government policies when the result is massive deficits. It is fair to ask why we need a discipline called economics if it excuses such obvious mistakes.

I argue that the economist must accept foursquare the reality of irrational choices and the social mistakes that result from those choices. I also argue that it is because—not despite—the proliferation of social mistakes that the economist can and must assume rational choice on the part of voters in presenting arguments to them concerning how they can improve their choices. Finally, I argue that it is in the context of widespread social mistakes that economists can operate on the basis of an ethical system that would command general acceptance were it articulated by economists in a fashion that the public could understand.

Some Social Mistakes

What are some examples of irrational choice in policy making? Let's begin with "project labor agreements" (PLAs). Many public construction projects require bidders to sign an agreement to hire union labor and follow union rules should they submit the winning bid. This is despite the fact that the vast majority of construction workers do not belong to unions. By requiring a PLA, government builders discourage nonunion contractors from bidding and force them to adopt costly union rules in the event that they do submit the winning bid. This has a record of increasing construction costs.

The irrational element in this is that pro-union government builders buy into the union line that, contrary to the evidence, PLAs reduce construction costs and prevent delays in construction. The "studies" done to support PLAs are shot through with false claims like this in support of their implementation (Tuerck 2010).

A related construction issue has to do with the "prevailing wage." The federal government and most state governments set the wages on government-sponsored construction projects at above-market levels. This is despite the fact that there is no rationality in requiring taxpayers to shoulder above-market costs when contractors could find workers to perform the projects more cheaply.

Next, consider the popularity of "Buy-American" laws that require government agencies to procure goods from an American firm even when the same goods are available at lower price from a foreign firm. Is it rational to require taxpayers to pay more for goods just because they are made in the United States?

Probably the best example of using economics to defraud the public is "modern monetary theory" (MMT). This is the notion that, because it controls the money supply, the federal government can spend all it wants as long it doesn't bring about inflation in doing so (Kelton 2020). It is unnecessary to impose taxes in order to pay for, say, infrastructure when the government can just print the money, instead. This argument ignores the role that taxes play in constraining the size of government. Just as it is necessary to charge consumers a price for buying a hamburger, it is necessary to charge them a price for infrastructure. Otherwise, government breaks the bond between voters and government. If government spends by printing money, it removes the constraint on its spending that taxes impose. The inflation that inevitably results from money creation is just the modern equivalent of government paying its debts "with a smaller quantity of silver than would otherwise have been requisite."

The public debt surpasses 100 percent of GDP at this writing. Legislation under consideration by Congress would drive the percentage higher. This can probably be laid to the influence that the proponents of MMT have had on elected officials.

Traditional welfare economics is predicated on the assumption that politicians choose rationally. Once we abandon that assumption, the road is clear to embracing an ethical system the only prerequisite for which is acceptance of the belief that efforts to induce voters to think rationally are welfare enhancing. Voters who think rationally will not support politicians who embrace PLAs, prevailing wage laws, Buy-American laws, or MMT.

Social mistakes are made by voters who make themselves susceptible to manipulation by politicians whose interests coincide only rarely with those of the voters themselves. I will argue that economists have a duty to apply whatever tools they have at their disposal to correct those mistakes. If that means applying a rational choice model whose assumptions are at odds with the very voter behavior that it is necessary to correct, then so be it.

CHAPTER 3

Where Economics Stands Today

The discipline of economics has an enormous presence in modern society. Hundreds of articles compete for the attention of thousands of academics employed to teach economics in college classrooms. Every year dozens of new books on economics fill the shelves of libraries and bookstores.

Yet, economics as practiced today has become a failed project. The economic downturn of 2007–2009 and then the downturn that was brought about by the COVID outbreak—along with the policies implanted in response to them—represent catastrophic failures in economic analysis.

Economics, nevertheless, also has logical and factual content of enormous value. The problem does not lie, therefore, with economics itself. The problem lies with the fact that economics is often misused by its practitioners. It is economists or people who pose as economists who have failed. And they have failed by not understanding that they have a two-fold mission. One mission is to articulate and test economic theories. The other is to identify and correct a willingness on the part of noneconomists to accept misdiagnoses of economic problems.

It will therefore be my thesis that economic advice is wasted unless presented in a manner that requires its audience to rethink its own predispositions and biases and to eliminate inconsistencies in their beliefs that impede rational thought and choice. If protective tariffs and usury laws continue in effect year after year, well that just illustrates the failure of economists to do their job.

It is only when it explains the grip of irrational thought *and* of sentiments on people's thinking that economics can be effective in promoting rational policies. The economist-preacher, like the missionary doctor, must convince his audience to reject the ideas in which they take sentimental comfort.

Smith and Sentiments

It is important to understand the role that sentiments played in the writings of Adam Smith and other contributors to the Scottish Enlightenment, principally Hume. Sentiments are, in this tradition, both important to the understanding of human behavior and quite orthogonal to rational thought. The contrast is dramatically evident in the existence of Smith's *Theory of Moral Sentiments*, on the one hand, and of *The Wealth of Nations*, on the other. Smith, in my view, came closer than any economist after to him to contrasting what he called "sentiments" with what I call "rational thought." This is not to say that there is some "Adam Smith problem" in reconciling the two works but that the two works complement each other, as identifying the conflicting forces at work in the human persona.

Emma Rothschild writes of how Smith and his contemporary, the Marquis de Condorcet, emphasized the importance of sentiment.

> The indefinite idea of sentiment was at the heart of Smith's and Condorcet's political and moral theory. Sentiments were feelings of which one is conscious, and on which one reflects. They were also events that connected the individual to the larger relationships in which he or she lived (the society, the family, or the state). The traffic of commerce of modern life was at the same time a traffic in opinions and sentiments (Rothschild 2001, 9).

As biographer Dugald Steward put it, Smith "was concerned with the 'principles of the human mind,' the 'principles of the human constitution,' and 'the natural progress of the mind'" (Rothschild 2001, 7). "Wonder, Surprise, and Admiration, are words, though often confounded, that denote in our language sentiments that are indeed allied, but that are in some respects different also, and distinct from one another," wrote Smith in "The History of Astronomy" (Smith 1982, 33).

This is the Smith who grounded economics in the principles of self-interest and the invisible hand and simultaneously regretted the "indolence" of landlords and the conspiracies among "masters" to suppress the wages of labor. It is the Smith who both analyzed and preached.

Like modern economists, Smith understood the importance of viewing economic systems in what we now call a "general equilibrium" framework, wherein people act out of self-interest and markets clear. But he also understood economic behavior in the broader context of "sentiment" as it motivated all behavior, including economic behavior. And he had his own values as they pertained to the unearned prosperity of landlords and the unfortunate condition of factory labor.

Stigler's condemnation of preaching could be seen as a condemnation of any temptation by economists to let sentiment, whether their own or someone else's, interfere with their work. I will not urge economists to let their own sentiments motivate them except insofar as their sentiments motivate them to be more effective in what they do. My principal argument concerning sentiment is that it is a motivator that economists cannot ignore if they want to be effective. Sentiment can work to the bad by undermining rational thought and therefore social progress, but it can also work to the good if it can be utilized to bring about rational choices.

The modern-day successor to 18th-century ruminations on senti-ments is the field called cognitive science, about which there is more to be said later. As with Smith, contributors to this field are focused on "the principles of the human mind." Although cognitive science is a blend of neuroscience and computer science, it has also commanded the attention of economists. As we will see, there is much in this field that bears on the role of economics in policy making.

Why should we try to come up with an effective way for economists to preach? Because, as I argue, economists must turn people away from wrongheaded sentiments. There is no point in working out economic analyses if voters and politicians are going to be deterred from responding constructively to what the authors of those analyses are saying.

Caplan's Pessimism

At the opposite extreme from the Stigler–Wittman utopianism is the pessimism conveyed by Bryan Caplan in his book, *The Myth of the Rational Voter*. Caplan argues, as I do, that policy errors are persistent and systematic. "Considering how many rational voting models are with us," he writes, "the scientific value of such models, has fallen close to zero"

(Caplan 2007, 208). But it is the task of the economist to correct for the irrationality that bedevils such models.

Caplan does not consider the idea that economists should find a way to get voters to think as the rational voter model assumes. He believes that if voters are not, in fact, rational, there is no point in assuming rational choice when modeling voter behavior. But suppose that economists were able to goad politically obtuse voters into thinking in terms of the rational choice model just as doctors might try to goad obese people into imagining themselves as well-toned physical specimens in order to motivate self-discipline. Are the efforts of these economists and doctors then wasted? My answer, as it applies to economists, is no. It is the principal mission of the economist to get voters and their elected representatives to think rationally.

The danger here is that the economist will confuse, as Jonathan Gruber did, what he thinks is good for the voter with what the voter, when pressed to think through his preferences, will realize is good for himself. It is only the latter question that the economist should consider.

In a 1993 article on "The Scope and Limits of Preference Sovereignty," economist Tyler Cowan comes close to what I wish to promote with what he calls "cleansed preferences"—preferences that are cleansed of bad information so that the decision maker is "fully informed about the world and in a clear state of mind" (Cowan 1993, 260). In fact, however, when I speak of the rational choice assumption, I am thinking of *how* people think, not whether they are fully informed *when* they think. There is a difference.

Cowan correctly argues against a need for the individual to "cleanse" his preferences before choosing. As he puts it, "the cleansed preferences standard fails to measure welfare accurately because so much of value in our lives arises from imperfect information" (Cowan 1993, 263). There is a subtle but important difference between the information on which we act when choosing and the degree of rationality that enters into our choices.

Three Mistakes That Economists Make

The economics profession, despite its immense presence in the college curriculum, in bookstores, in popular culture, and on the Internet, has marginalized itself in three important ways. First, economists have become so absorbed with their own philosophical battles that they have forgotten their audience—the everyday voter trying to make sense of the cacophony of messages he gets from politicians and special pleaders, many armed with economic arguments crafted to assure that the voter will not take a rational stance toward questions of economic policy.

A group of economists with whom I have much sympathy—the Austrians and their allies—have, unwittingly I think, contributed to this unhappy state of affairs. This they have done by branding the neoclassical model as an instrument in the service of collectivism rather than an instrument that serves to promote rational thought. By abandoning economics in favor of philosophy, the Austrians have turned themselves into academic curiosities, speaking to each other in their own special language, providing their audiences with delightful, iconoclastic riffs on society but, in the end, having no influence over the actual course of events. More about this later.

There are two additional ways that economists have succeeded in caricaturing themselves. One is by functioning as opportunists who will provide evidence that supports any proposition, however absurd, provided that the incentives—power, money, tenure—are sufficient. The other is functioning as metaphysicians, whose business it is to create a dialogue over the implications of a priori principles, purely arrived at and conceived in such as a way as to exclude any thought of how their efforts inform public discourse. Both groups—the opportunists and the metaphysicians—are content in their roles, insofar as they can make a living and enjoy a degree of prestige and intellectual stimulation doing what they do. The opportunists and the metaphysicians have but one common trait—that they have given up on any wish to make economics effective for positive societal change.

Economists have come to this pass because they have, as a group, ignored the fact that they must speak to the greater public, not themselves. In particular, they have ignored the methodological style of the Scottish Enlightenment. Smith, who, along with Hume, is the leading figure of that school of thought, had the right idea of what economists should do. And that is to induce people driven by sentiment into making rational choices about the political world in which they live and work.

In his essay on "The Methodology of Positive Economics," Milton Friedman offered the following optimistic assessment of economics:

> I venture the judgment ... that currently in the Western world, and especially in the United States, differences about economic policy among disinterested citizens derive predominantly from different predictions about the economic consequences of taking action—differences that can be eliminated by the progress of positive economics—rather than from fundamental differences in basic values (Friedman 2008, 147).

Now, almost 70 years later, such "progress of positive economics" as we have seen does nothing to validate Friedman's optimism. This is largely owed to the declining authority of the rational choice paradigm in economic discourse. That paradigm, already under assault from heterodox, dissenting schools of economics, took another hit when the U.S. economy slid into a downturn in 2007. Here the fault lay not with the dissenters but with proponents, whose "always-in-equilibrium" characterization of the economy was shown to be questionable. Economists who continue to write in the rational choice tradition do themselves and everyone else no favors when they promise that the economy can never fall into a protracted slump.

My methodology is instrumentalist in approach. The job of the economist is to frame issues in a fashion that induces people to make rational choices. I pointed out earlier that I would attempt to fashion an ethical system within the rules of which economists could more effectively apply their recommendations to public policy. Ironically, this system requires economists to use people's sentiments against their inclination to ignore sound economics and to be manipulated by unsound economics. The ethical system recommended here is one in which the economist strives to make his listeners translate the implications of economics into their own ethical systems in order to find and correct flaws in those systems that prevent them from choosing rationally on policy issues.

I undertake this task on the basis of one and only one ethical premise: that the individual should make policy and political choices on the basis of his own internally consistent analytical framework and that, where this framework is not internally consistent, he should identify the inconsistencies and eliminate them.

Economist Don Ross takes the opposite course. According to Ross, "the core of the humanist rejection of neoclassicism is the belief that people who acted like, and exclusively like, economic agents would be morally and pragmatically dubious specimens of their kind." According to Ross, "most economists (including university-based economists) make their living as practical consultants, not as theorists." Thus "most economists professionally act as though they assume that people are rational fools" (Ross 2005b, 150).

> One crucial fact that cannot be ignored ... is that the working methodology of microeconomics, and its associated basic pedagogy, has shown much greater stability than have its high-level theoretical commitments. ... This leads to the suspicion that either economic practice, or economic theory, are intellectual *games*, in the pejorative sense: on the first interpretation, theory is something that practitioners need not really take seriously, while on the second interpretation the practice is a con job, unmasked by theorists, that economists will willfully pursue until policy makers wake up and stop paying for it (Ross 2005b, 215).

In fact, the con job is the one perpetrated by theorists like Ross who try to eliminate any consideration of rational choice by policy makers.

CHAPTER 4

Neoclassical Economics and Its Critics

Neoclassical economics emerged out of a centuries-long debate over two issues: (1) What constitutes proper economic activity and (2) how do we measure value? The "marginalists" of the 1870s finally developed an approach under which consumer choice determined what constituted proper economic activity and under which value could be derived from the subjective preferences of consumers. There was, until that time, an insistence that certain kinds of economic activity were to be eschewed as socially harmful and that value originated with the labor content of goods. The marginalists' emphasis on consumer sovereignty put an end to all of that.

Economic Thought Leading up to the Neoclassical School

Goring back over the ages, we see a far different picture. On the matter of socially harmful economic activity, Aristotle contrasted the "art of money-making" with the "art of managing a household" (Aristotle 1951, 13–20). To be sure, certain forms of money-making were an acceptable part of household management. These were, according to Aristotle, "necessary and honorable." On the other hand, retail trade is "justly censured, for it is unnatural and a mode by which men gain from one another." Among the various types of money-making, "the most hated sort, and with the greatest reason, is usury, which makes a gain out of money itself, and not from the natural use of it" (Aristotle 1951, 20).

Thus, Aristotle ensured that usury would be condemned for many generations to come.

Sixteen centuries later, St. Thomas Aquinas documented "the sins which have to do with voluntary exchange." These are of two major types: "fraud committed in buying and selling" and "usury taken on loans" (Aquinas 1950, 53).

Following Aristotle, Aquinas observed that:

> there are two kinds of exchange. One may be called natural and necessary, by means of which one thing is exchanged for another, or things for money to meet the needs of life, and this kind of trading is not the function of traders, but rather of household managers or of statesmen, who have to provide a family or a state with the necessities of life. The other kinds of exchange is that of money for money or of things for money, not to meet the needs of life, but to acquire gain … . Now the first kind of exchange is praiseworthy, because it serves natural needs, but the second kind is justly condemned, because, in itself, it serves the desire for gain, which knows no limit but extends to infinity (Aquinas 1950, 63).

The second topic over which philosophers—and then economists—grappled is how to measure value. Adam Smith tried to deal with the fact that some goods, like diamonds, had a high market price while others, like water, did not.

> The word VALUE, it is to be observed, has two different meanings, and sometimes expresses the utility of some particular object, and sometimes the power of purchasing other goods which the possession of that object conveys. The one may be called "value in use;" the other, "value in exchange." The things which have the greatest value in use have frequently little or no value in exchange; and on the contrary, those which have the greatest value in exchange have frequently little or no value in use (Smith 1976a, 32).

Smith went on to expound upon the "diamond-water paradox." "Nothing is more useful than water: but it will purchase scarce anything." On the other hand, "a diamond … has scarce any value in use; but a very great quantity of other goods may frequently be had in exchange for it" (Smith 1976a, 33). Value, for Smith, also depended on the quantity of labor that it took to make a good. "Labor alone . . . never varying in its own value," said Smith, "is alone the ultimate and real standard by which the value of all commodities can at all times and places be estimated and compared" (Smith 1976a, 37).

Smith was particularly sympathetic to the role labor was condemned to play in the factory system: A man working in a factory comes to spend his whole life:

> in performing a few simple operations, of which the effects too are, perhaps, always the same, or very nearly the same, has no occasion to exert his understanding, or to exercise his invention in finding out expedients for removing difficulties which never occur. He naturally loses, therefore, the habit of such exertions, and generally becomes as stupid and ignorant as it is possible for a human creature to become (Smith 1976b, 303).

No hesitancy there to preach!

Smith's successor, David Ricardo, is probably best remembered for his theory of comparative advantage, which he illustrated in terms of two countries and two commodities, the cost of which was determined entirely by their labor content. "Possessing utility," Ricardo wrote, "commodities derive their exchangeable value from two sources: from their scarcity and from the quantity of labor required to obtain them." For some commodities (works of art and rare wines), their value is determined "by their scarcity alone."

> These commodities however form a very small part of the mass of commodities daily exchanged in the market. By far the greatest part of those goods which are the objects of desire are procured by labor; and they may be multiplied, not in one country alone, but in many, almost without any assignable limit, if we are disposed to bestow the labor necessary to obtain them (Ricardo 1911, 6).

Thus, Ricardo had what Stigler called "a 93 percent theory of value."

In the 19th century, Karl Marx developed a theory of value under which labor generated a surplus (production over and above that needed to pay the worker), which the capitalist expropriated. This expropriation of surplus value, said Marx, would ultimately lead to the overthrow of capitalism and the emergence of a "dictatorship of the proletariat."

Because only labor was able to generate surplus value in his system, Marx was unable to reconcile three key features of his system, that: (1) the rate of surplus value (labor surplus divided by wages) would be the same across sectors, (2) the organic composition of capital (ratio of capital to labor) would vary across sectors, and (3) the profit rate would be the same across sectors. In Volume 3 of *Das Kapital*, his coauthor Friedrich Engels tried unsuccessfully to resolve this "great contradiction," leaving it to the neoclassical school to do so later, with its total abandonment of the labor theory of value.

Marx's ideas, however energetically he would have denied it, turn out to have their origin in theology. The "essence of the argument" by the medieval scholastics (or "school men"):

> was that payment may properly be demanded by the craftsmen who made the goods, or by the merchants who transport them, for both labor in their vocation and serve the common need. The unpardonable sin is that of the speculator or middleman, who snatches private gain by the exploitation of public necessities. The true descendent of the doctrines of Aquinas is the labor theory of value. The last of the Schoolmen was Karl Marx (Tawney, 2015, 48).

The notion that value derives from labor thus has a history that began well before Marx. Aquinas' admonitions against usury were part of a broader condemnation of what was to become capitalism.

The Neoclassical School: Changing Everything

The neoclassical school began with the publication in 1871 of Carl Menger's *Principles of Economics*, along with, in the same year, William Stanley Jevons' *Theory of Political Economy*, and in 1874, Léon Walras' *Elements of Political Economy*. Jevons read Richard Whatley, a cleric, as a young boy. Whately argued that "it is not that pearls fetch a high price because men have dived for them; but on the contrary, men dive for them because they fetch a high price." Whately also argued that economics should be renamed *catallactics,* the "science of exchanges" (*New World Encyclopedia*).

Jevons wrote:

Repeated reflection and inquiry have led me to the somewhat novel opinion, that value depends entirely upon utility. Prevailing opinions make labor rather than utility the origin of value. I show, on the contrary, that we have only to trace out carefully the natural laws of the variation of utility, as depending upon the quantity of commodity in our possession, in order to arrive at a satisfactory theory of exchange, of which the ordinary laws of supply and demand are a necessary consequence (Jevons 1879).

He went on to say, "it is clear that Economics, if it is to be a science at all, must be a mathematical science."

I hesitate to say that men will ever have the means of measuring directly the feelings of the human heart. A unit of pleasure or of pain is difficult even to conceive; but it is the amount of these feelings which is continually prompting us to buying and selling, borrowing and lending, laboring and resting, producing and consuming (Jevons 1879).

So this is where the world had gone by the late 19th century. Proscriptions against usury or speculation were no longer taken seriously among economists. Our feelings, though immeasurable, prompted us to borrow and lend. Value depended on utility, not labor. The modern era had arrived.

The neoclassical model emerged out of the writings of several contributors, notably, besides Jevons, Menger, and Walras, Francis Edgeworth, J.B. Clark, Vilfredo Pareto, and Frank Knight. The whole edifice was fairly much in place when Knight published *Risk, Uncertainty & Profit* in 1921 and in doing so fleshed out the idea of perfect competition (Knight 1921, 76–86).

In the neoclassical model, competition is "perfect" insofar as no buyer or seller can affect price by varying the amount bought or sold. The price of any good or input to production adjusts until the quantity supplied equals the quantity demanded (and thus we have "equilibrium economics"). Individual consumers adjust their consumption to the point at which the amount they are willing to pay for one more unit of any good equals its price. Producers adjust production to the point at which price equals the cost of producing one more unit. Firms adjust their labor force to the point at which the wage rate equals the value added to production by the last unit of labor. They adjust their holdings of capital to the point at which the cost of capital equals the value added to production by the last unit of capital. Thus, labor and capital become coequal in their importance to production and the distribution of income. In the neoclassical model, the labor theory of value loses all credibility as an analytical tool.

The neoclassical model became the principal tool for determining how policy changes affect economic activity. Does the government want to impose a tax on cigarettes? Well, assuming that it will collect the tax from cigarette producers, the tax will increase the cost of both producing and buying cigarettes. By increasing cost, the tax will cause a reduction in the quantity of cigarettes bought and sold. A portion of the tax will be borne by producers and a portion by consumers, the difference depending on the willingness of either party to absorb the burden.

Studies Based on the Neoclassical Model

The economist estimates this willingness as manifested by the responsiveness of producers and buyers to a change in price. Once this is known, the economist can estimate the effect of the tax on the price received by the producer, net of tax, the price paid by the consumer, and the substitution of one brand for another. One study found that an increase in the cigarette tax paid by Chicago area residents would bring about "a substitution toward high-tier cigarettes and in tar, nicotine, and carbon monoxide consumed per pack" (Chiou and Muehlegger 2014, 621).

We could ask, also, about the effects of increasing the minimum wage. Neoclassical analysis shows that the minimum wage will increase the cost of employing the existing labor force and, as a result, induce employers to lay off current workers, perhaps hire new, more productive workers, and raise prices. A recent example is the analysis by the Congressional Budget Office (CBO) of a proposal to raise the federal minimum wage to $15.00 per hour. The CBO found that

- From 2021 to 2031, the cumulative pay of affected people would increase, on net, by $333 billion;
- Employment would be reduced by 1.4 million workers, or 0.9 percent;
- The number of people in poverty would be reduced by 0.9 million.
- Real gross domestic product (GDP) would fall slightly (CBO 2021).

Another topic is government spending on infrastructure. At this writing, there is a proposal nearing agreement for Congress to increase infrastructure spending by $550 million. There is another, more controversial, bill to increase infrastructure spending by $3.5 trillion.

There have been many studies of the costs and benefits of government infrastructure. According to one study, which summarized the literature on this topic, a 1 percent rise in the value of the public sector capital stock would increase productivity by 0.03 percent (Holz-Eakin and Mandel 2015). In 2018, U.S. government fixed assets were $15,058, and GDP was $20,580 billion. So, by that estimate, $100 billion in new spending on infrastructure would increase GDP by $4.1 billion.

Cost–benefit analysis also falls under the rubric of neoclassical economics. In 2004, the Beacon Hill Institute (BHI) undertook a cost–benefit analysis of a proposal to build 130 wind turbines in Nantucket Sound off the coast of Cape Cod (Haughton, Giuffre, Barrett, and Tuerck 2004). The wind turbines would have been placed in federal waters where they were immune from the draconian zoning laws that regulate every kind of construction on the shores surrounding them. The project would, by necessity, have been highly subsidized were it to go forward. This is because wind power, especially when provided from an offshore platform, is far more expensive than power provided by fossil fuel sources.

BHI determined that the economic costs of the project, in present value terms, would have come to $947.2 million and the economic benefits (including environmental benefits) to $735.5 million (Haughton, Giuffre, Barrett, and Tuerck 2004, 4). Ultimately, the project fell through when its sponsor failed to get financing even after the state legislature authorized above-market rates for power generated by the turbines.

Next, we can consider the effects of taxes and subsidies on individual incentives to work, save, and invest. One example is income and payroll tax rates and their effects on the quantity of labor offered in production. The task of estimating the effect of a change in these tax rates on the supply of labor involves the calculation of the elasticity of supply of labor, that is, the percentage decrease in the supply of labor that results from a 1 percent decrease in the after-tax wage rate. One extensive review article found this to be 0.31 for men and 3.6 for women (Keane 2011, 1071). If the wage rate is $10.00 and a 50 percent tax reduces the after-tax wage rate to $5.00 per hour, the supply of male workers will shrink by 15.5 percent.

Government transfer payments to individuals can also reduce the supply of labor. In his book, *The Redistribution Recession*, Casey Mulligan estimated the reduction in labor supply that resulted from expansion in the safety net programs that was instituted by the Obama administration during the contraction of 2007–2009 (Mulligan 2012). Mulligan's hypothesis was that by making means-tested benefits more generous, the government had reduced the incentive to work. He estimated that the expansion of programs like food stamps and unemployment insurance increased the fraction of their income that people could recover by not working by 8 percent. This caused labor supply to fall by 3.389 billion hours over this period (Tuerck 2021, 154).

The neoclassical model also accounts for the fact that what are called accounting profits are better construed as costs. Suppose a corporation considers the purchase of a machine costing $1,000. In order to buy this machine, it needs $1,000 in financing, which it chooses to raise by issuing stock. Suppose that in order to get investors to provide that much in financing, it must offer them an annual after-tax return of at least 15 percent on their stock purchase. Without taxes, the cost of capital would be 15 percent. But suppose that the tax rate on corporate income is 20 percent and the tax rate on dividends is 10 percent. The corporation must then generate $208.33 in annual profits on the purchase of the equipment in order to induce people to buy the stock. (This ignores the tax saving from depreciation.) Of the $208.33 in profits, 80 percent, or $166.66, remains after taxes to pay stockholders in dividends. Of that amount, 90 percent or $150 remains as after-tax dividends received by the stockholder, which yields the 15 percent return needed to get him to buy the stock.

The taxes on profits and dividends raise the cost of capital from 15 percent to 20.83 percent. If the machine yields a return less than 20.83 percent, the machine won't be worth buying. The higher cost of capital will discourage the corporation from buying the machine.

But who bears the tax? It may seem obvious that U.S. shareholders will bear the tax. But U.S. shareholders have the option of investing their money anywhere in the world. They will simply, therefore, move their money out of the United States to other countries where they can purchase shares that pay at least 15 percent after taxes. That means that the burden of the tax will be shifted onto U.S. workers as U.S. corporations invest less in U.S. plant and equipment. One study of German corporations found that workers bear about 40 percent of the corporate tax burden (Fuest, Peichl, and Siegloch 2015).

The Austrian Diversion

Earlier in this book, I noted Lionel Robbins' definition of economics as "the science which studies human behavior as a relationship between ends and scarce means which have alternative uses." Robbins saw economics as aimed at solving what has come to be known as the "means–ends problem." I prefer to see economics as "the science that studies the means–ends problem *as a societal phenomenon*." Someone else can study Crusoe's choices on the island before Friday arrives. Economists get called into action after Friday arrives.

The purpose of this book, as frequently stated, is to make economics effective for encouraging rational choice in policy making. Economists can make a difference if they are willing to goad people into abandoning folk economics and acting rationally.

They can't make a difference, however, if they abandon the means–ends problem as the focus of their work. Yet, there is a strand of thought in economics that argues for doing just that. I call this the Austrian diversion since it is the wellspring of Austrian economic thought. Says one Austrian:

> Robbins's conception implicitly presupposes a given knowledge of ends and means and reduces the economic problem to a technical problem of mere allocation, maximization or optimization, subject to certain restrictions, which are also known. In other words, Robbins's concept of economics reflects the essence of the neoclassical paradigm and can be considered completely foreign to the methodology of the Austrian school as it is understood today (de Soto 2008, 5).

James Buchanan is a towering figure in the recent history of economic thought. He received the Nobel Prize in economics in 1986 largely for his work in public choice, which can be understood as the application of economic theory to political behavior.

In his presidential address before the Southern Economic Association, entitled "What Should Economists Do?" Buchanan foreshadowed the Austrian attack on Robbins. Buchanan constructed a classroom situation in which a student is asked to distinguish between an economic and a technical problem. The student answers in terms of the standard, means–ends dichotomy provided by Lionel Robbins: The consumer has an economic problem—a limited budget to allocate between competing uses. The engineer, on the other hand, has a technical problem—he need only apply his budget to one use, for example, building a dam to certain specifications. This answer pleases the teacher, who subscribes to Robbins' definition but not a rebellious student in the back row, who says, "'But there is really no difference'" (Buchanan 1964, 216).

Buchanan argues that the first student in his example errs by failing to understand that the problems faced by consumer and engineer alike are both purely technical. We can reduce the consumer's problem to the standard means–ends framework provided only that the consumer, like the engineer, knows what he wants. Once we agree that both decision makers have a clearly defined problem, the only difference, according to Buchanan, is that the consumer wants to maximize utility and the engineer wants to meet the specifications of the dam. There is, in either case, a unique "mechanical" solution to the problem.

"If I know what I want," Buchanan says, "a computer can make all my choices for me. If I do not know what I want, no possible computer can derive my utility function since it does not really exist" (Buchanan 1964, 217). Robbins, Buchanan argued, went astray by putting the problem of resource allocation at center stage. Resource allocation, Buchanan further argued, was more an engineering problem than an economic problem. What economists should study is exchange or "catallactics" (Buchanan 1964, 214). Ironically, this was in the spirit of Richard Whatley, who inspired the very utility-maximization paradigm that Buchanan rejected.

In *The Austrian School: Market Order and Entrepreneurial Creativity,* Jesús Huerta de Soto ascribes a similar argument to the Austrian school of economics, with which Buchanan had a philosophical connection. For de Soto, the gulf between Austrian methodology and the Robbinsian means–ends problem was even greater. The means–ends problem is, for de Soto, to be banished from the study of economics: "Thus for Austrians," he says,

economics is not a set of theories on choice or decision at all, but instead it is a theoretical corpus which deals with processes of social interaction, processes which vary in their degree of coordination depending upon the alertness that actors show in their entrepreneurship (de Soto 2008, 4–5).

He goes on:

Robbins portrays man as an automaton, a simple caricature of a human being, who may only react passively to events. In contrast with this view, Mises, [Israel] Kirzner and the rest of the Austrian school maintain that man does not so much allocate given means to given ends, as constantly seek new ends and means, while learning from the past and using his imagination to discover and create the future (via action) (de Soto 2008, 5).

What, then, we must wonder, is a consumer doing when he strolls down the aisle in the hardware store looking for a set of tools. He presumably has some budget for this purchase and presumably has competing uses for that budget. Shall he buy the electric screwdriver and the handsaw or the manual screwdriver and the power saw? This is certainly a means–ends problem and certainly falls within the purview of the neoclassical paradigm. Buchanan would hand this problem over to the engineer. Unfortunately, the engineer won't be interested.

The reason that the consumer-in-the-hardware-store problem is a matter for the economist to consider is that it is the economist who must speak out on government policies that will affect how much the consumer has available to spend when he enters the hardware store, along with the items and prices that are there for him to consider. Taxes and regulations affect the choices made by the hardware store concerning what to offer for sale and the choices made by the consumer concerning what to buy. In analyzing those taxes and regulations it is important to understand how the consumer makes choices. The neoclassical model provides the framework for that analysis.

Thus, Buchanan is further off the mark when he writes: "Almost at the other extreme from the Crusoe models, the refinements in the theoretical model of perfectly competitive general equilibrium have been equally, if not more, productive of intellectual muddle," he says. Such models are "the dry-rot of postulated perfection" (Buchanan 1964, 218). Economists given to mathematical modeling are prone to look on market order as a *means* of accomplishing the basic economic functions

> that must be carried out in any society. The "market" becomes an engineered construction, a "mechanism," an "analogue calculating machine," a "computational device," one that processes information, accepts inputs, and transforms these into outputs which it then distributes (Buchanan 1964, 219).

The passage shows just how far economists have gone astray in understanding what it is they should do. It hardly matters, first of all, how people engaged in mathematical modeling look at markets. What we know is that many economists, whether they engage in mathematical modeling or not, look at markets as a means to achieve political, not economic, ends—and frequently with unhappy results. We also know that politicians are prone to using the technical support provided to them by economists in order to advance policy goals to which voters are prone irrationally to acquiesce.

The problem is not whether someone engages in mathematical modeling or builds a model based on perfect competition and on the existence of a general equilibrium. The problem is whether policy choices are made on the basis of good modeling or bad modeling and how politicians respond when confronted with modeling results.

De Soto, like Buchanan, complains that neoclassical theorists "assume that ends and means are given and view the economic problem as simply a technical problem of optimization" (de Soto 2008, 9). This leads to a criticism of the use of mathematics in economics.

> Mathematical formalism is particularly suitable, . . . for expressing the equilibrium states neoclassical economists study, but it does not permit us to incorporate the subjective reality of time, much less entrepreneurial creativity, both of which are essential features of the analytical discourse of Austrian theorists (de Soto 2008, 11).

The condemnation of mathematics doesn't end there. Even rationality itself is unneeded.

> For the same reason, Austrians also regard neoclassical economists' axiomatic criteria of rationality as senseless. Indeed, if an actor prefers A to B and B to C, they [sic] may very well prefer C to A, without ceasing to be "rational" or consistent, if they have simply changed their mind (if only during the hundredth of a second that they think about the issue). For Austrian economists, the usual neoclassical criteria of rationality confuse the concepts of constancy and consistency (de Soto 2008, 12).

At this point, one is left wondering just what Austrians mean by "consistency," if indeed that concept holds any meaning at all for them. It appears that the economist who would apply the tools of neoclassical economics to policy issues puts himself in league with socialists. "The factors which make socialism theoretically impossible … are the very factors which explain why empiricism, cost–benefit analyses and utilitarianism in its strictest interpretation are not feasible in our science" (de Soto 2008, 12).

This is because there are no objective "facts" on which to ground empirical analyses. "For Austrians, cost is the subjective value the actor attaches to those ends they give up when they decide to pursue a certain course of action." For Austrians, "there are no objective costs" (de Soto 2008, 10). Indeed,

> there are no directly observable, objective events in the outside world. According to the Austrian subjectivist view, the objects of research in economic science are simply the ideas that others hold about what they do and the ends they pursue (de Soto 2008, 13).

What we have, therefore, is an economic philosophy, the practitioners of which want to declare the entire corpus of policy research to be illegitimate. Indeed, the very idea of conducting research on policy issues is philosophically impossible inasmuch as policy makers base, or purport to base, their decisions on "observable, objective" data.

The broader issue is whether the perfect competition (or "equilibrium") model is so bereft of content that economists should be embarrassed by turning to it. To read Buchanan or de Soto on this issue is to discover that perfect competition entered the economic lexicon as an act of sabotage.

The guiding principle of Austrian theory is that there can be no understanding, or even consideration, of economic behavior outside the marketplace. It is only the market that can coordinate the myriad of subjective interests that individuals bring to bear on the exchange of goods and only the market that can determine the price at which goods are bought and sold. Because there is no single, organic public to consider, it is always illegitimate to speak of some public good or goods whose optimal provision is the goal of policy. Economics is about action, not choice, and the only action that can be addressed in the context of economic theory is action that takes place at the level of the individual in the marketplace, unfettered by government intrusion. In writing on subjectivism in Austrian economics, Edward Stringham tells us that "in addition to rejecting utilitarianism, the most thoroughgoing subjectivists reject other attempts to create proxies for societal well-being such as monetary income, migration patterns, or cost–benefit analysis" (Stringham 2010, 64).

The problem is that voters and the people they elect use these very proxies to make choices, whether thoroughgoing subjectivists like it or not. In turning their noses up at the use of such proxies, the Austrians simply concede the playing field to those policy makers who would act without any regard to the axioms of rationality. The same subjectivists who would sit out the debate on whether a public project passes a cost–benefit test would be the first to complain if the project, as a *public* project, were approved.

The Austrians have marginalized themselves by ignoring the problem faced by their audience—which is how to make the political choices before them. The Austrians have become victims of their own success. Having destroyed the intellectual case for socialism, they are rather like the occupying troops of a defeated but restless country that they never wanted to occupy in the first place. Because of their antipathy to mathematical modeling, the Austrians have compromised their ability to contribute in any practical way to the solution of the very phenomenon—the expansion of the welfare state—which they so fervently oppose.

Some Austrian economists dabble in the idea that the marketplace is so efficient that government may be largely if not entirely unnecessary (Stringham 2011). The marketplace alone will provide, if we just let it. For these economists, it is not that government performs efficiently or inefficiently. It is that societies perform efficiently in the absence of government—or at least where we find evidence of workable anarchy— *because* of the absence of government. Thus, libertarianism meets Marxism in advocating the withering away of the state. I find all this to be very unhelpful for the purpose of injecting rational thought into such government as we have. We should change the conversation from one in which we condemn the inefficiency with which government is fated to operate (or in which we dismiss the need for government at all) to one in which we recognize existing inefficiencies in government and then adopt a strategy for reducing them.

The most important contribution of the Austrian school was to the socialist calculation debate (Boettke 1999). In several works, Friedrich Hayek and Ludwig von Mises showed that central planning fails because of the inability of individual buyers and sellers to communicate their subjective preferences to the central planners. Because people cannot articulate all they know, the planners can never organize economic activity in the required top-down manner.

That argument is as compelling now as it was during the 1930s, decades before central planning collapsed in the Soviet Union and its satellite states. The problem that lies in discouraging politicians from attempting to manage the economy from the top-down, however, is that they do not see their efforts, taken alone, as moving the country toward socialism. At least until very recently, there has been no major political party in the United States that would overtly endorse socialism and no serious candidate for national office who would join such a party.

The problem, as argued above, is that politicians adopt policies that voters would not approve, were they to think and choose rationally. This leaves the economist with the task of goading politicians into recognizing and owning up to the deficiencies in the policies they adopt. If they followed the logical conclusions of de Soto's argument, Austrians would sit out this process. Their message therefore amounts largely to a counterproductive distraction.

De Soto provides a passage in which he draws a straight line from Adam Smith to Marxism. Smith, he alleges, paved the way for Marxism through his labor theory of value. Moreover, "Smith flooded economic science with Calvinism, for example, supporting the usury provision and distinguishing between 'productive' and 'unproductive' occupations." Smith introduced a "lukewarm 'liberalism'" that paved the way for today's social democracies (de Soto 2008, 35).

De Soto also finds the "general equilibrium model" a source of mischief. The problem began with Paul Samuelson's formalization of economics in the language of mathematics, which Samuelson saw as paving the way for market socialism. Equally addicted to mathematics, Samuelson's Chicago School protagonists defended the free-market model in terms of their "equilibrium-always" approach.

This inclination of the Austrians to interpret economic methodology solely in terms of the ideological agenda to which that methodology might be applied undermines their claim to credibility. Contrary to the Austrians, the general equilibrium model is merely a method of thinking systematically about how an economic system reacts to changes in policy and to other events that occur outside the assumed boundaries of the system itself. It can indeed be a tool in the hands of either the critics or the defenders of the free market. The question, though, is how to employ the model to the end of producing better policy. The Austrians embarrass themselves when they condemn a methodology that would frequently serve to impugn the very interventionist policies they so stridently oppose.

It is especially revealing to see Smith branded as a deviationist. De Soto's argument borders on fanaticism, not unlike we can see in the life of Ayn Rand, who might well have been the 20th century's most avid defender of capitalism. In her book, *Atlas Shrugged,* Rand charted the gathering in a mountain refuge of a collection of industrialists who decided that they had had enough of collectivism and would go on strike—remove themselves from the job of keeping the economy going—and simply let the world around them implode. Rand, who was hugely successful as an author, refused to associate with anyone daring enough to challenge her principles. We are reminded of how one of Rand's acolytes rushed home to burn his collection of Brahms records, when Rand deemed Brahms to be musically unacceptable. Would de Soto's students be advised to burn their copies of *The Wealth of Nations?*

There are Austrians who consider it a public service to engage in littering and who would eliminate any legal protection against libel. There are others for whom the Pirates of the Caribbean is not a movie but a model for voluntary exchange.

I would be the first to agree that there is a place for off-the-wall theorizing, inasmuch as caricature can be a useful rhetorical style in the classroom. The pity is that the very economists who exposed the failure of socialism would strip themselves and their allies in the neoclassical school of the tools that are needed to resist the growing encroachment of socialism on the American psyche.

Raising Keynes

The Austrian attack on neoclassical economics is of minor importance compared to the attack that came from John Maynard Keynes, with the publication in 1936 of his *General Theory of Employment, Interest, and Money*. Keynes' attack was explicitly directed at what he called "classical" economics by which he meant not only the works of Smith, Ricardo, and J.B. Say, but also the more recent works of the neoclassicals (Keynes 1936). Say was an important target for having been charged with responsibility for the admonition, "supply creates its own demand," much denigrated by Keynes in his attack.

Out of Keynes' book came the eventual division of economics into "macro" and "micro" fields, macro encompassing Keynes and subsequent authors who have written in his tradition, and micro encompassing neoclassical economics and its tradition. It may be true that Austrian economics spans both fields, though contemporary Austrians, particularly Hayek and Mises, were united in their criticism of Keynes.

Keynes published his book in the depths of the Great Depression and intended, in writing it, to dispel the grip that "classical" economics had on economic thinking. His argument was that, while classical economics held that economic downturns were self-correcting (à la Say), the Great Depression, which began in 1929, was certainly not. The problem was that there could emerge a state of affairs in which both goods and labor were in excess supply and in which price and wage adjustments were inadequate to correct the imbalance. If supply creates its own demand, the economy is always in equilibrium. If it does not, if, in particular, supply can exceed demand, then the economy suffers a disequilibrium in which workers cannot find jobs and firms cannot find customers.

Once the economy falls into this kind of a slump, it would be up to the government to correct the matter. One approach would be to reduce interest rates. Another, probably more effective, approach would be the "socialization of investment," which is to say more government spending (Keynes 1936, 378).

Keynes' core theory rested on the existence of a "marginal propensity to consume" (MPC) out of disposable income. In the (neo)classical system, saving fuels investment and is thus expansive for its effect on economic activity. In the Keynesian system, saving is a "leakage" out of the spending stream and thus contractive for its effect on economic activity. The MPC comes into play in considering how another dollar of government spending will affect the overall economy, as measured by "real," inflation-adjusted GDP.

In the neoclassical model, more government spending simply diverts resources from personal consumption to government. But in the Keynesian model, where resources are underemployed, more government spending expands the economy by more than the increase in spending. This is because the government spending leads to an increase in disposable income out of which consumers will spend some fraction (the MPC), thus adding further to the disposable income of other consumers and further rounds of increased spending.

Keynes speculated on the magnitude of the MPC, suggesting at one point that it might equal 0.6. Thus, if, say, the government spends another billion dollars, it will immediately add that amount to disposable income, leading the recipients of that increase in disposable income to increase their spending by $600 million, and the recipients of that increase to increase theirs by $360 billion, and so on until the economy ultimately expands by $2.5 billion.

1. $\Delta \text{GDP} = \$1 \text{ billion} + 0.6 \times 1 \text{ billion} + 0.6^2 \times 1 \text{ billion} + \cdots$
$$+ 0.6^n \times 1 \text{ billion} = \$2.5 \text{ billion},$$

where $n \to \infty$.
Or

2. $\Delta \text{GDP} = \$1 \text{ billion} \times \dfrac{1}{1 - 0.6} = \$2.5 \text{ billion}.$

There is a government spending multiplier of

3. $K_G = \left(\dfrac{1}{1 - \text{MPC}} \right) = \left(\dfrac{1}{1 - 0.6} \right) = 2.5.$

By spending $1 billion more, the government can expand the economy by $2.5 billion.

There is also a tax multiplier, calculated as

4. $K_T = \dfrac{-\text{MPC}}{1 - \text{MPC}}.$

In the current example, given a tax cut of $1 billion,

5. $\Delta \text{GDP} = \dfrac{-0.6 \times \left(-\$1 \text{ billion} \right)}{1 - 0.6} = \$1.5 \text{ billion}.$

This formulation has proved to be very powerful, in large part because it provides a method for stimulating the economy without depending on wage and price adjustments that may not be forthcoming in a shrunken economy. Thus, government is able to expand the economy simply by spending more or, in a broader formulation, taxing less. Textbook treatments of Keynes identify spending increases and tax reductions as expansive for their effects on the economy, and spending cuts and tax hikes as contractive.

One question, however, is how often do we need the Keynesian model? When we consider the recent history of U.S. economic activity, the answer is "not very often." The purpose of the Keynesian model is to provide tools for increasing real GDP when actual real GDP is below potential (full-employment) real GDP. On average, over the period 1949 to 2019, actual real GDP was only 2.6 percent less than potential real GDP. Of the 280 calendar quarters over this period, only 52 were marked by recessions. This suggests that full employment is more the norm than is less-than-full employment and that the need for Keynesian remedies is rare (Tuerck 2021, 280).

Another, more fundamental, question is whether the Keynesian model correctly accounts for individual economic behavior. Suppose again that the government cuts taxes by $1 billion or equivalently passes out $1 billion in welfare checks. Is the individual economic agent hardwired, as Keynes argues, to spend some fraction of that (and, hence, to save the remaining fraction)? Or does he engage his utility-maximizing calculus to determine what fraction to spend? The neoclassical model sees the choice as coming from the individual's utility-maximizing calculus. The individual will want to spend (and save) in such a way as to maximize lifetime utility.

Seen through that lens, the individual is unlikely to want to spend as much as 60 percent of the resulting increase in his disposable income. According to the neoclassical model, people try to adjust their consumption and saving in such a way as to spread their consumption evenly over their lifetimes. It makes no sense to spend most of any temporary increase in disposable income at the moment it is received, given the decreasing marginal utility of income. If Eve hit the lottery for $1 million, would she want to rush out and spend $600,000 right away, or would she want to put most of the money in saving with a view toward spreading the benefits of her winning more evenly over the rest of life? Neoclassical economics argues that she would put most of the winning into saving. Then, if the account yielded 5 percent annually, she would increase her current spending by $50,000, not $600,000, thus leaving enough money in place to fund the same modest but still significant increase in consumption in the coming years.

This analysis suggests that the multiplier associated with tax cuts and spending increases conducted as a stimulus exercise during an economic downturn is likely to be small. In the current example, it is only 0.05.

Thus, for example, the $800 billion "stimulus" package enacted to rescue the U.S. economy from the recession of 2007–2009 manifested itself mainly in increased saving, not consumption. It produced little or no stimulus to the economy (Tuerck 2021, 242–243).

This brings us to current times and current thinking about the relevance of neoclassical economics to a world in which people often violate the assumptions from which it is derived. We take that up next.

CHAPTER 5

The Irrelevance of Economic Assumptions

The main attack on neoclassical economics comes from behavioral economics. Leaders in this field, notably, Daniel Kahneman and Amos Tversky, have found from experiments that people do not conform to the precepts of rational choice theory. While the behaviorists are therefore damaging to the optimism of Stigler and Wittman, they are at the same time—and ironically—conclusive as to the importance of the rational choice model. I will explain why later.

There have been other criticisms to the rational choice model, one of which questions whether there is such a thing as the individual who thinks rationally. John B. Davis writes of the postmodernist critique, which undermines the self "as a self-subsistent real entity" (Davis 2003, 7). As an alternative to that view of the self, Davis propounds a doctrine of "collective intentionality" (Davis 2003, 193).

Descartes and His Critics

In 1637, Rene Descartes set the stage for a debate over the question whether mind and body were separate entities. For Descartes, the mind is distinct from the body. In his book, *Mind: A Brief Introduction,* John R. Searle sketches the efforts since Descartes to purge philosophy (and science) of this dualism. Descartes's conception of a subjective soul or mind housed in an objective body ran afoul of the materialism that came to be the dominant philosophy. "There is a sense," writes Searle, "in which materialism is the religion of our time, at least among most of the professional experts in the fields of philosophy, psychology, cognitive science, and other disciplines that study the mind" (Searle 2004, 34).

In his survey of the materialist reaction against Descartes, Searle first identifies "methodological behaviorism," whereby the study of the mind is meaningful only in terms of those actions that could be observed as responses to external stimuli (Searle 2004, 35). For the behaviorists it was unnecessary to consider the ontological basis of mind, independent of the body, inasmuch as it was only observable behavior that mattered.

Critics fault the rational choice model from the point of view of cognitive science, much of which consists of a program aimed at overturning Cartesian dualism (and about which there will be more commentary later). The critics aim to establish that there is no mental "I" separable from the material "I." Don Ross and Paul Dumouchel regard dualism as "the hypothesis that ends the world" (Ross and Dumouchel 2004, 264).

The rational choice model assumes the very sort of dualism that these critics abhor. Economic agents, defined as individual buyers and sellers, make willful choices that cannot be explained by the physiology of the brain. Cognitive science will not tolerate this willfulness. We cannot admit of any process in which people reason their way toward a decision. Thus, people cannot be economic agents.

But other creatures can.

"A good example of a prototypical economic agent," says Don Ross, "is an insect." This is because the insect does not possess any kind of free will worth talking about. "Because the relations between an insect's goals and its behavioral responses are hardwired and sensitive to environmental variations along finitely specifiable and tightly stereotyped dimensions, insects are ideal subjects of microeconomic study" (Ross 2005b, 251).

This leaves nothing of the purposeful behavior identified by economist Ludwig von Mises in *Human Action*. "Reason and experience," said Mises, "show us two separate realms: the external world of physical, chemical, and physiological phenomena and the internal world of thought, feeling, valuation and purposeful action" (Mises 1949, 18). This emphasis on the autonomy of the individual decision maker at the "whole" person level—this dualism—is taboo in cognitive science.

Cognitive science presents a theory of the mind akin to one that Friedrich Hayek offered, though with different results. Like Hayek, Don Ross presents a theory according to which thoughts emerge without any central decision-making unit "at the top" to direct them. Whole "selves" are the result of emergent and spontaneous choices at the subpersonal level. Ross defends this conceptualization on the argument that there is no central "self" and that the individual as an autonomous chooser is nonexistent.

Emergent selves may well be stable but, they are often stable around badly made choices relating to certain issues, particularly issues involving the community. "Selves" show a lot of stability when it comes to business choices. The problem is that, when it comes to public policy choices, stability is far less attainable.

Ross wants to abandon methodological individualism in favor of his idea of economic agency, whereby agency operates at the subpersonal, not the personal, level. This book aims to restore methodological individualism around the notion that agency can be made to operate at the personal level by triggering an awareness of inconsistencies that beleaguer personal choice.

The methodological individualism embraced here takes the position that economics speaks to a purposeful, autonomous economic agent, who is the person. That economic agent will have a varying ability to choose rationally depending on the problem presented to him. Politicians typically do not want economic agents acting in their capacity as voters to choose rationally at all and therefore present arguments to voters in a fashion that is aimed at limiting their ability to choose rationally. It is typically in the interest of politicians to undermine rational thought.

Reference Dependency

Another dissenting school is neuroeconomics, which seeks to unite economics, psychology, and neuroscience into a unified discipline aimed at explaining how people choose. One prominent practitioner of this discipline has found that there exists a mechanism in the brain whereby people transform "objective values" into "subjective factors" in a manner that makes irrational choices unavoidable. This happens because of a phenomenon called "reference dependency": Because the brain does not encode the objective values of the outside world, people (and animals) cannot make choices on the basis of all the relevant facts, independently of how those choices are presented to them. They must choose on the basis of whatever context it is in which the choice is presented (Glimcher 2011).

A goal of economics is, inasmuch as possible, to free economic decision making from this reference dependency. As I write, there is ongoing discussion over whether the U.S. corporate tax rate should be increased from 21 percent to 28 percent. The fact that this discussion is reference dependent stems from the treatment of the existing rate, which is 21 percent, as the rate against which to compare the new rate (28 percent). But the correct question is what the rate should be, given that it could be 5, 21, 28, or 90 percent. The existing rate has no particular importance in answering that question. One job of the economist is to rescue policy discussions from reference dependency and to focus them on the broader issues before policy makers.

I take issue with neuroeconomics to the extent that it does not give adequate attention to the ability of people to unlearn bad choices. I also take issue with the argument made by Caplan that there are rational explanations for irrational behavior. If people behave in a self-destructive fashion and if their inclination to do so is not irrational on its face, then rationality has no meaning.

Economics is called upon to explain two different phenomena requiring two different methodological approaches. One phenomenon is "private choice." Behavioral economics and neuroeconomics focus on explaining how individuals choose, given exogenous constraints on their ability to choose—how, for example, an individual chooses whether to play the lottery or to take up using crack cocaine. The other phenomenon is "social choice," in which individuals make choices that affect the constraints under which they and other individuals make choices. If a resident of Portugal chooses to consume a bottle of wine, he is engaging in private choice. If, by contrast, he chooses to restrict the importation of English cloth, he is engaging in a social choice.

It is appropriate, where possible, to employ the tools of behavioral economics or neuroeconomics to explain either private or social choice. Both private and social choices are shot through with irrationality. There is one difference between private and social choice, however, in that there is scant reason to employ the "folk economics" discussed in the Preface to influence private choices. On the contrary, people have been using folk economics for centuries to influence social choices.

No individual resident of Portugal would typically try to influence a citizen's decision to buy a bottle of wine by employing economics. We can, on the other hand, fully expect Portuguese cloth producers to come out in force with an argument claiming that, because Portuguese labor costs are lower, it makes no sense to import English cloth—the argument that Ricardo refuted with his explanation of comparative advantage.

This is not to say that folk (which is to say, irrational) arguments never come up in private choice. Nowadays, there are substantial efforts underway to get people to use "green" energy and "fair trade" coffee and to quit smoking. Folk arguments deployed to influence social choices (mandate green energy, eliminate "unfairly traded" coffee from the university cafeteria, and ban smoking) do spill over into private choice.

Emboldened by recent successes, fans of behavioral economists have asserted the declining usefulness of neoclassical economics (or, as here, "equilibrium theory"):

> The problem with equilibrium theory is that it makes certain assumptions—perfect competition, perfect information, perfect rationality—that behavioral economists have discovered (and most lay people have long known) are not true. Competition is not perfect, people do not have complete information, and we do not make rational choices. What behavioralists … want to know is how human irrationality in markets alters market balance (Shermer 2008, 98).

It is not surprising that years before this assessment appeared in print, Lionel Robbins declared behavioral economics to be a "queer cult" (Robbins 1932, 87).

Questioning the Assumptions

Mainstream economics does assume that economic actors or "agents" are rational. There are several tests of rationality, one of which is whether agents are consistent or "transitive" in their choices (as addressed by de

Soto earlier). If a consumer chooses Budweiser over Coors and Coors over Miller, then, to be rational, he must choose Budweiser over Miller. This is necessary in order for an economist to predict how the consumer would respond to a change in any of the factors, such as price or income, that influence his choice of beer.

Another test is nonsatiation, which is to say that an economic agent always prefers more to less of any economic good. Two beers are better than one. Three beers are better than two.

Next, the principle of diminishing marginal utility says that the additional utility that an agent gets from another unit of some good will be less than what he got from the previous unit.[1] This relates to the question how much better the first beer is than the second and how much better the second is than the third, and so on. By explaining the idea of diminishing marginal utility, Jevons rescued economics from the long-accepted premise that value derives from the amount of labor it takes to produce a good.

Finally, there is the assumption of completeness. By this assumption, agents have a preference ordering that extends to every conceivable combination of goods. A patron knows whether he prefers having a shepherd's pie at the local Irish pub or ribs at his preferred barbecue restaurant. He also knows whether he prefers caviar at Le Bernardin on West 51st Street in New York City or the grilled octopus at Il Gattopardo on West 54th— just in case he could afford either.

There are also rationality assumptions that pertain to options involving risk. According to mainstream utility theory, people make choices between options involving risk by assigning utilities to them and then picking the option that confers the highest expected value, measured in terms of utility.

Suppose, for example, the agent has a choice between receiving $460 with certainty or playing a game that offers a 60 percent chance of

---

[1] Strictly speaking, this assumption should be written as the "law of diminishing marginal rate of substitution": The amount of money I am willing to spend on the third beer is less than the amount I am willing to spend on the second, and the amount I am willing to spend on the second is less than the amount I am willing to spend on the first.

winning $100 and a 40 percent chance of winning $1,000. The mathematical expectation of this game is

(1) 0.6($100) + 0.4($1,000) = $460.

If the agent played this game over and over again, his average winning would converge to $460.

Now suppose also that the same person knows how much utility he would get by winning $100 and how much he would get by winning $1,000. Specifically, he would get 10 utilities from winning $100 and 80 utilities from winning $1,000. Then his expected utility (E(U)) from playing the game would be

(2) E(U) = 0.6(10) + 0.4(80) = 38.

Finally, let's assume that his utility would be 35 if someone just gave him $460 on the understanding he would not play the game. But then he will want to play the game. The utility from playing the game (38) exceeds the utility (35) from receiving the amount ($460) equal to the game's mathematical expectation. The player would, on this account, be identified as risk seeking.

Players can also be risk averse. Suppose the utility of a $460 payout was 40. Then the agent would agree not to play the game in exchange for that payoff since the utility from not playing exceeds the expected utility from playing.

In mainstream analysis, variations in the probability of a gain (or loss) do not independently affect E(U). Experimentation has shown, however, that the agent can go from being risk seeking to risk averse or the other way around as the probability of winning (or losing) changes. This discovery has given rise to prospect theory, under which people are risk averse when it comes to monetary gains but risk seeking when it comes to losses.

In this regard, consider the "independence" assumption. Specifically, consider a choice between (A) winning $10 million with certainty or (B) winning $10 million with a probability of 90 percent, winning $30 million with a probability of 9 percent, and winning $0 with a probability of 1 percent. The question, in game (X), is which option, (A) or (B), will the individual choose?

Now consider game (Y) in which the choices are (C) winning $10 million with a probability of 10 percent and winning $0 with a probability of 90 percent and (D) winning $30 million with a probability of 9 percent and winning $0 with a probability of 91 percent. Now the question is, in game (Y), which option, (C) or (D), will the same person choose?

Economist Maurice Allais once posed a similar question to a group of economists (Lewis 2017, 258–259). For a game similar to (X), most chose (A). For a game similar to (Y), most chose (D). These choices seem plausible enough. In game (X), it is easy to see why a person would choose (A) over (B). By choosing (A), the person loses the chance to win far more than he could by choosing (B), but he also avoids the chance of winning $0. On the other hand, in game (Y), where the probability of winning anything is small, it seems plausible that the person would prefer option (D), which offers the chance of winning a far larger amount, albeit with a lower probability than that offered by option (C).

The problem, however, is that this pair of choices would violate an assumption—the independence assumption—which must be satisfied in order to choose rationally. Let's see what that means. If the agent chooses (A) over (B) in game (X), then, in order to choose consistently, he should choose (C) over (D) in game (Y). That's because both options eliminate a 90 percent chance of winning $10 million. By choosing (D) over (C), the individual violates the independence assumption. When the probability of winning is very low (here 9 percent), the agent will choose the option with the lower probability of winning but larger return from winning.

Now let's consider more examples, adapted from a multiauthor book on neuroeconomics (*Neuroeconomics: Decision Making and the Brain 2009*, 148). Table 5.1 illustrates situations in which people are typically risk seeking or risk averse, depending on the probability of winning a bet. For example, Joe would have to receive $15 in order to forgo a gamble in which his expected gain is $10 (= 0.01 × $1,000) and is, in that fashion, risk seeking. On the other hand, he would have to receive only $850 to forgo a gamble in which his expected gain is $900, making him risk averse.

Table 5.1 Risk seeking and risk taking

	Gains for Joe	**Losses for Mary**
Low probability	(1) G(1,000, 0.01) = $15 Risk seeking	(2) G(–$1,000, 0.01) = –$12 Risk averting
High probability	(3) G($1,000, 0.90) = $850 Risk averting	(4) G(–$1,000, 0.90) = –$800 Risk seeking

Now let's consider Mary. She would pay $12 to avoid a gamble expected to cost her $10 (= 0.01 × $1,000) and is thus risk averse. Yet she would pay only $800 to avoid a gamble that is expected to cost her $900, making her risk seeking.

These examples illustrate real-world decision making. For example, case (1) applies to gambling, when the probability of winning is small. Case (2) applies to insurance, where the probability of losing is small. Case (3) applies to the choice of certainty in the Allais game (X), and case (4) to the choice of risk in a game when the probability of losing is high.

There is yet another way in which the individual can behave irrationally. This comes under the label "hyperbolic discounting." Suppose that you have two choices to make: (A) accept a gift of $1,000 now or (B) $2,000 in a year and (C) accept a gift of $1,000 in 10 years or (D) $1,100 in 11 years. Experiments show that you would probably choose (A) over (B) but (D) over (C). Right now, you would forgo a return of 100 percent that you would get by waiting one year for your gift. But, looking ahead 10 years, you would delay the same gift by waiting a year when the return would be 10 percent. The fact that you are impatient enough now to forgo a rate of return of 100 percent but unwilling to forgo a rate of return of 10 percent several years from now says that you are engaging in "hyperbolic discounting."

Now let's consider a more complicated example. You have an asset that will pay out $1,000 in 25 years, but you want to get what you can by selling the asset now. What would you expect to be paid? Rationality requires you to calculate the present value of the $1,000 payoff and to charge that amount.

To make the necessary calculation, you would need to know the discount rate for financial assets bearing similar risks. Suppose that the applicable discount rate is 5 percent. Then we can calculate the present (or current) value of the future payout as

$$(3) \quad PV(E) = \$1{,}000e^{(-0.05)25} = 286.50.$$

You should not be willing to sell the asset for less than $286.50. Suppose, alternatively, you calculate present value as

$$(4) \quad PV(H) = \frac{\$1{,}000}{1 + 25} = \$38.46.$$

Now your minimum payment is much lower. Equation (3) is based on exponential discounting, whereas equation (4) is based on hyperbolic discounting, which applies a much higher discount rate to near-term choices than to more distant choices. To see that, imagine you plan to sell the asset in 25 years, at which time it will mature. Now the applicable formulas are

$$(5) \quad PV(E) = \$1{,}000e^{(-0.05)0} = \$1{,}000.$$

and

$$(6) \quad PV(H) = \frac{\$1{,}000}{1 + 0} = \$1{,}000.$$

As the length of time from the current moment to the time when the asset matures becomes greater and greater, PV(H) gets closer and closer to PV(E), as illustrated in Figure 5.1.

Now another example: In 1981, Kahneman and Tversky described an experiment in which they posed this question to a group of students: A disease will break out that could kill 600 people. There are two programs to curtail the spread of the disease. Which treatment program do you prefer (Tversky and Kahneman 1981, 453)?

- Program (1):
  - A. 200 people are saved.
  - B. There is a 1/3 probability that all 600 people will be saved and a 2/3 probability that none will be saved.

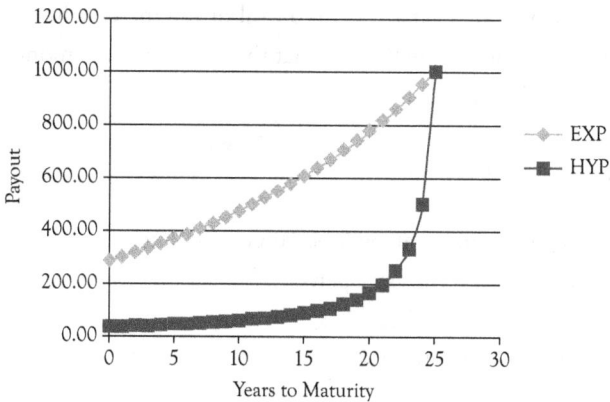

Figure 5.1 Payouts with exponential and hyperbolic discounting

- Program (2):
  - C. 400 people will die.
  - D. There is a 1/3 probability that nobody will die and a 2/3 probability that 600 people will die.

The result was that 72 percent of the students picked A over B, and 78 percent picked D over C. Yet A and C are identical for their consequences for the hypothetical patients.

This illustrates the "framing problem" in behavioral economics. The implication of this experiment is that it is possible to frame a policy question in such a way as to get a hoped-for response. In this case, it means deciding, first, whether the subjects of the survey are risk averse or risk taking. Compare (A) with (C). Both provide identical outcomes. The same goes for (B) and (D). If a respondent, in program (1), chooses (A) over (B), he is choosing certainty over risk, that is, displaying risk aversion. But, if in program (2), he chooses (D) over (C), he is choosing risk over certainty, that is, displaying risk taking. The experimenter can use this information to get the outcome he prefers.

As a further example, consider the possibility that someone hopes to reduce the unemployment rate through an increase in the money supply. He knows that there will be objections based on the existence of a "Phillips curve," which is to say a negative relationship between the unemployment rate and the inflation rate. The question is how to frame the issue in order to get majority approval of the increase in the money supply and to get it despite the fact that the increase in the money supply is inflationary. The data show that

Without monetary expansion,

1. The unemployment rate will be 10 percent, and
2. The inflation rate will be 2 percent.

With monetary expansion,

1. The unemployment rate will be 5 percent, and
2. The inflation rate will be 4 percent.

Thus framed, experiments show that the choice will be in favor of monetary expansion.

Now let's reframe the problem.

Without monetary expansion,

1. The employment rate (the faction of job seekers who are employed) will be 90 percent, and
2. The inflation rate will be 2 percent.

With monetary expansion,

1. The employment rate (the faction of job seekers who are employed) will be 95 percent, and
2. The inflation rate will be 4 percent.

Now the choice will be against monetary expansion. Why does reframing the question shift the vote away from monetary expansion? The answer lies in the "ratio difference equation." The ratio of the unemployment rate without monetary expansion to the unemployment rate with monetary expansion is 2 (=0.10/0.05). This makes monetary expansion look like a strongly effective policy. On the other hand, the ratio of the employment rate with monetary expansion to the employment rate without monetary expansion is 1.06. This makes monetary expansion look less effective.

Now the question arises whether the irrational decision making illustrated here makes any difference to the economist in his effort to perform his mission. We define that mission as helping noneconomists better understand the social choices before them. The value of economics lies in its ability to inform decision makers of the consequence of their actions in a way that induces the decision maker to choose consistently.

Unfortunately, a great deal of attention has gone, instead, to the question of whether economics is—or should be—considered a science. And that question has turned largely on still another question—whether the legitimacy of an economic theory depends on the realism of its assumptions or whether it depends, instead, on the accuracy of its predictions.

The foregoing review of findings in behavioral economics focused on the argument that the assumptions on which mainstream economics rest are false. Mainstream economics assumes that the independence axiom holds true in choices involving risk, that people are exponential discounters, and that framing doesn't matter to people's choices. But, in a famous essay, cited earlier, Milton Friedman argued that it is the accuracy of a theory's predictions that matters, not the accuracy of its assumptions. By that reasoning, it wouldn't matter if preferences, say, were intransitive as long as a theory that assumes transitivity correctly predicts that a decrease in price will lead to an increase in quantity demanded.

Friedman argued that economics should aspire to the practice of "positive science." The task of economics, as such, "is to provide a system of generalizations that can be used to make predictions about the consequences of any change in circumstances." Much like Stigler, Friedman wrote that "positive economics is in principle independent of any particular ethical position or normative judgments" (Friedman 2008, 146).

Friedman went on to cite the goal of achieving a "living wage" as emblematic of a consensus on "basic values." He offered the argument for a minimum wage as an example. Differences of opinion about the minimum wage, he said, are "largely grounded on an implicit or explicit difference in predictions about the efficacy of this particular means in furthering the agree-on end." Proponents argue that the minimum wage reduces poverty by raising the wages of the poor.

Opponents argue that it increases poverty by leading to job losses. But there is hope for progress.

> Agreement about the economic consequences of the [minimum wage] legislation might not produce complete agreement about its desirability, for differences might still remain about its political or social consequences; but given agreement on objectives, it would certainly go a long way toward producing consensus (Friedman 2008, 147).

As noted above, Friedman's hopefulness was ill-founded. There is not enough agreement about "objectives" in the world today to foster an environment in which economics can be used to narrow differences between contending factions on the direction of economic policy. Sadly, those differences seem only to be widening and, in the process, leaving the discipline of economics in shambles.

Let's return to Friedman's view of science. "The ultimate goal of a positive science," he wrote, "is the development of a 'theory' or 'hypothesis' that yields valid and meaningful (i.e., not 'truistic') predictions about phenomena not yet observed" (Friedman 2008, 148). But the view that we can test the validity of a hypothesis by the conformity of its assumptions to reality is "fundamentally wrong and productive of much mischief" (Friedman 2008, 153). And that is not all: "Truly important and significant hypotheses will be found to have 'assumptions' that are wildly inaccurate descriptive representations of reality, and, in general, the more significant the theory, the more unrealistic its assumptions (in this sense)" (Friedman 2008, p. 153). The assumption that the leaves on a tree seek maximum sunlight is wildly inaccurate (since the leaves can't "seek" anything), but it nevertheless does a good job of predicting how the leaves arrange themselves.

Friedman's article triggered a *methodenstreit* in the 1960s and shows up today in discussions of economic philosophy and methodology. Probably the most forceful attack came from Paul Samuelson in the 1963 *Papers and Proceedings* of the American Economic Association. Samuelson registered particularly strong disapproval of Friedman's argument that it is legitimate to assume perfect competitions, even when competition is not "perfect," provided that in doing so we can make valid predictions. For example, it would be ok, said Friedman, to assume perfect competition in the cigarette industry if doing so led to correct predictions of the consequences for that industry of an increase in the cigarette tax.

Samuelson interpreted what he labeled the "F-Twist" as part of the general effort by Chicago School economists, of which Friedman was a leading figure, to use perfect competition as a tool to advance the Chicago free-market agenda (Samuelson 1963, 233). For Samuelson, the notion that valid predictions could flow from invalid assumptions was patently false.

We can illustrate his point of view by considering the oft-quoted syllogism: "All men are mortal. Socrates is a man. Therefore, Socrates must be mortal." Here the statement "All men are mortal" is an assumption—the so-called major premise. The statement "Socrates is a man" is another assumption—the minor premise. The conclusion (or prediction) is "Socrates is mortal."

Samuelson correctly argued that in all such syllogisms the assumptions imply the conclusions and are implied by the conclusions. The conclusion that Socrates will die follows from the assumption that he is mortal, but it is also true that the conclusion that he will die implies that all men are mortal.

Returning to economic theory, consider the question of how a tax on cigarettes would affect the price and quantity of cigarettes. Neoclassical theory predicts that the tax will cause price to rise and quantity sold to fall, ceteris paribus (everything else being equal). But what about things that might not be equal, which is, to say, unchanged? Suppose, for example, that cigarettes are a "Giffen good," a good so critically important to the consumer that, in making the consumer feel poorer, the rise in price brought about by the tax causes him to buy more cigarettes. If our assumptions falsely exclude this possibility, the theory would fail to predict accurately.

The underlying justification for Friedman's example of a tax on cigarettes consists of the fact that we could estimate the effects on price and quantity by assuming perfect competition *and* that cigarettes are not a Giffen good. This could be true even if the cigarette industry is not perfectly competitive, simply because the cigarette manufacturers don't respond differently than they would if perfect competition prevailed.

Because we cannot know if the market for a product satisfies all the assumptions we make in studying it, we have to settle for the results we get. One cut at a prediction might yield better results than the previous cut, simply because the economist was more thorough in his assumptions the second time around (allowing, say, for an increase in the availability of black-market cigarettes).

There is no need for economists to avoid making assumptions that do not fully correspond to reality in making predictions about the effects of tax changes or other policy changes. There is also, to be sure (and contrary to Friedman's argument), much to be gained if assumptions that fit the problem more exactly also lead to better predictions. The proof will always be in the pudding. Do the assumptions made in predicting an outcome lead to the most accurate predictions or would other assumptions do better?

Friedman's argument, made in the 1950s, well before behavioral economics became the giant influence that it is now, provides a strong defense of neoclassical economics. If the neoclassical assumptions need not be realistic, why worry that they aren't?

Thus, the neoclassical program retains its viability, at least in the academic literature. It turns out that one leader in the behavioral movement has defended the omission of behavioral economics from introductory economics textbooks. "There are good reasons," he says,

> for keeping prospect theory out of introductory texts. The basic concepts of economics are essential intellectual tools, which are not easy to grasp even with simplified and unrealistic assumptions about the nature of the economic agents who interact in markets. Raising questions about these assumptions even as they are introduced would be confusing, and perhaps demoralizing (Kahneman 2011, 286).

We must ask, however, why we would want to encourage college students to trust theories that are based on palpably wrong assumptions. Could it be that the assumptions don't matter?

CHAPTER 6

Ideology

Ideologies are not simply lies; they are truthful statements about what a man thinks he sees.

—Joseph Schumpeter

One way to induce a politician to change his position on some issue is to erode his confidence in the way he is perceived by his constituents and peers for taking the position he takes. The economist brings about this result by putting out an analysis, based on the rational choice model, that is sufficiently compelling to make the politician realize that he is seen as having no defense against the analysis.

This contradicts the usual characterization of the behavior of politicians and of the power of economists to influence their behavior. The idealized, textbook conceptualization of the politician has him seeking advice from economists and other experts in order to serve the public interest. As characterized here, the politician may believe that he cares, and wishes to be perceived as caring, about the public interest, but his goal is to protect the ideological packaging in which he has wrapped his appeal to the electorate.

What the politician can—and must—do is choose positions on specific issues that he can defend on the basis of his self-chosen ideology. Ideologies are not separated by rigid lines from each other, and politicians are free to mix and match. Thus, otherwise left-leaning Jimmy Carter and Ted Kennedy famously sponsored deregulation during the late 1970s. Yet the politician must have at his disposal a coherent defense of whatever positions he chooses to take on the issues. Those positions will hinge in part on the degree to which taking his positions makes him electable and on the degree to which he feels comfortable defending the positions he takes on ideological grounds. Once identified with his positions on the issues, though, the politician cannot easily switch sides. He cannot easily go from "pro-deregulation" to "anti-deregulation" or from "pro-life" to "pro-choice." He thus finds himself having to defend a position he may prefer to abandon.

Enter the Economist

This is where the economist comes in. The economist subjects the politician's positions to tests selected from neoclassical economics. If it turns out that the politician's positions don't hold water, then the economist will have no recourse but to play on sentiments to get the politician to change his mind—if necessary, to embarrass the politician into changing his mind.

Campaign strategists provide the politician with ammunition to protect his positions from being tarnished by economists. Politicians seldom admit or even believe that they were wrong on an issue, but they do understand that others can see them to be wrong if they are unable to refute analyses showing that they are. In order to avoid being perceived as wrong, they will come to make some adjustment in a position they had previously taken.

Thus, a politician may have to recognize that the minimum wage law he supported is causing him to be seen as responsible for growing teenage unemployment. Not wishing to repeal the law or to admit that he irrationally supported it in the first place, he will search for some way to repair his image without repealing the law. He may come to favor an amendment to the law that exempts teenagers or to support a summer jobs bill funded by taxpayers. This he will defend by saying that it was his intention all along to create job opportunities for teenagers. He will not admit to choosing his new position because he discovered that the original law was causing teenagers to be unemployed but because he discovered a greater good that could be achieved by modifying that law while preserving the "spirit" of the original law.

The skillful politician will thus be able to take credit for an improvement in a law that he supported in its original form and that could, in its original form, have easily been seen as likely to cause the problem that necessitates the improvement. This, again, is because politicians don't succeed or fail according to the substantive mistakes they avoid or make but according to their ability to manage perceptions.

As long as he can keep his constituents and peers focused in this way on his good intentions, it won't matter how much damage the politician does by supporting a law in its original form. It won't matter that the minimum wage he supported causes workers to lose jobs. What will matter is that, having tacked one way in order to shore up wages, he was alert enough to tack the other way, to protect jobs.

The trick, then, is for the politician to be seen as a steward of the economy, rather than a person who risks destroying jobs by manipulating the wage rate. There is always enough uncertainty about the economy that no policy change can be easily blamed for having caused an unwanted outcome. Thus, politicians immunize themselves from accountability and political risk.

The only way the economist can rectify this state of affairs is to shake the politician's confidence in his constituents' willingness to buy into his rationalizations of his own actions. The only way to do that is, in this instance, to raise the question of why the politician undertook to set wages in the first place.

So why do voters elect politicians who support the minimum wage, given that it arguably causes workers to lose jobs?

People who support minimum wage laws typically assert that it is important that everyone enjoy some minimum standard of living and, on that basis, dismiss arguments about job losses as beside the point. Some such people might recognize the job losses brought about by the law as unwanted collateral damage, but they would feel it inappropriate to oppose the law inasmuch as doing so would be perceived as an abandonment of the crucial, overriding principle at stake. Here again, it is perceptions or, more generally, sentiments that drive behavior, not reality.

People support or oppose laws for many reasons, many of which may conflict with each other. But once a person has latched on to whatever ideology it is that implants itself in his mind, his support or opposition will remain largely unshaken, whatever the proven consequences of the law. The committed ideologue will not re-engineer his thinking on the basis of evidence bearing on whether the law should be passed or, if passed, repealed. The most he will do is support some modification in his original position that is made to appear as a course correction rather than an admission of wrongheaded support for a poorly conceived position.

Economists cannot therefore ordinarily hope to bring about major changes in public policy. They cannot get supporters of the minimum wage to see it as wrongheaded, rather than merely harmful in how it affects labor markets. They cannot expect voters to ask why their elected officials ever thought that it was their job to set wages in the first place.

Let me hasten to say that there have been instances in which economists have effected important change. The repeal of the British Corn Laws in 1846 was an important policy change and one attributable, as everyone recognized, to Ricardo. The Full Employment Act of 1946 was important and part of the legacy of Keynes. The Reagan tax cuts of 1981 and 1986 are frequently attributed to economist Arthur Laffer. But these are rare exceptions to the rule that politicians don't want to be compelled to make meaningful policy decisions on the basis of economic analysis.

Major policy changes ordinarily happen because of dynamics that lie beyond the control of economists. All that an economist can ordinarily do is influence the policy environment at the margin. And when major changes do occur it is rare for economists to receive credit for having predicted or engineered them, even when that credit is due. More importantly, it is rare for people to draw any lesson from the policy change at all, much less reflect on what the change says about competing economic theories.

Hayek and Mises argued persuasively in the 1920s and 1930s that central planning was impossible. The collapse of the Soviet Union in 1991 seems by any standard to have proved them right. Russia's rejection of central planning, along with its surrender of political control over Eastern Europe, brought about the most dramatic exercise in economic reorganization in history. Other countries have embraced capitalism by default if not through any change in official dogma. China and Vietnam embrace capitalist principles with a vengeance.

Yet, the Marxist dogma on which Soviet Russia was founded and to which China and Vietnam still pay homage has not lost its grip on the minds of millions of people. Marxists continue to manifest themselves in the halls of academe, the streets of Seattle, and a few third-world capitals. The world did not interpret the fall of Communism as reason enough to send Marxism into the dustbin of history, to which it should be confined, along with Ptolemaic principles of planetary movements or arguments for the existence of phlogiston.

To be sure, it is an oversimplification to assume that the great struggle today is between the remnants of Marxism and the capitalist paradigm. Few supporters of the minimum wage feel kinship toward the mob that stormed the Winter Palace. There are many ideologies that compete for the hearts and minds of the masses and their leaders. And politicians, especially American politicians, go out of their way to eschew any ideological attachment. Although this is always a smokescreen for the actual ideology that motivates them, it testifies to the wish by most voters to be respected as having "open minds" on the issues.

Political choices generally boil down to choices between two candidates. And ideologies group themselves into polar opposites. We can reach back hundreds of years and find the ideological currents and crosscurrents that run through the current stream of ideas and reduce them to two broad models of economic organization. Under the first model, which we can call the "free-market model," economic choices are, except in rare instances where government intervention is justified, best made by individual economic agents, correctly informed of opportunity costs and protected in their rights to private property. Under the second, which we may call the "collectivist model," the state (or church or other central authority) makes those choices for its subjects, leaving it to individuals to make private choices for themselves and to enjoy the benefits of private property only insofar as doing so is consistent with the goals of the collective.

Neoclassical economics interfaces with these choices in two ways. First, it provides a method of explaining economic behavior as it would take place under the free-market model and of providing a guideline for the appropriate degree of such government intervention as may be justified. Second, it stands as a critique of government intervention. As applied to the free-market model, neoclassical economics explains how the marketplace leads individual economic agents toward economic efficiency and the circumstances under which government intervention is needed in order to correct for externalities and other deviations from economic efficiency. As applied to government intervention, it shows how the state, by the very substitution of its goals over those of the individual, compromises the ability of individual economic agents to achieve efficiency in their interactions with each other.

In an earlier chapter, we saw how the "perfect competition" model provides a guideline to rational economic choice. In this model, individual economic actors are constrained by market-determined prices of goods that they buy and sell. Consumers are also constrained by budgets and workers and other suppliers of factor services by the limits on their time, energy, and access to financial capital. Firms are constrained to cover costs and, in doing so, to hold losses to zero. The firm that bets wrong on the cost of inputs or on the demand for its product or services goes out of business. The consumer and firm are tightly constrained in their choices by the necessity of avoiding insolvency.

It is important to understand that the perfect competition model does not encompass all that is to be said about the choices between opposing ideologies. In particular, it does not provide any explanation of the role of innovation under the free-market model or of how innovation comes to be suppressed under collectivism. It is correct, I think, to stipulate that the literature on innovation lies outside the domain of what I am taking to be "mainstream economics," which I equate with neoclassical economics. This is an important literature, and many of its contributors would criticize neoclassical economics for not encompassing it. Perfect competition describes, at best, commodity and financial markets in which homogenous products or financial instruments are bought and sold by a large number of buyers and sellers.

It is also important to understand that "perfect competition" is just a conceptualization of a market and, as such, has no ideological connotation. The model predicts that the market will produce an equilibrium price at which buyers and sellers have exploited all opportunities for mutually beneficial gain. Barring externalities such as air pollution, the outcome will be a socially optimal one.

We have seen that the circumstances under which people (and other creatures) make choices determine the degree to which those choices are likely to be rational or not. The tighter the constraints under which they choose, the greater the likelihood of choosing rationally.

There is an asymmetry in the rational choice model, as it is commonly presented. Consumers may choose destructive behavior patterns under the rubric of "rational addiction," but firms are constrained to maximize profits or perish.

Addiction is not rational. A model could be constructed to reflect any given set of prior restrictions on what does and does not constitute rational choice, including a restriction that rules out addiction. Once the restrictions, and the mechanism for enforcing them, were identified, all that would remain would be to derive the conditions for achieving the necessary, constrained optimization. The solution would be optimum within the specified constraints, but it is the constraints that would compel rational choice as defined in terms of the value system on which they were imposed.

Is it rational to use crack cocaine? To engage in binge drinking or casual sex? To listen to rap? One cannot answer except in terms of one's own sentiments as they relate to such practices. All, with the exception of rap, threaten the life of the person engaging in them, much as failure to minimize cost threatens the life of the firm. Other practices—sloth, overspending, nagging one's spouse—are less immediately threatening but carry their own penalties in terms of the resulting reduction in the quality of life.

Parents do, with varying degrees of success, constrain their children's choices before giving them access to whatever the market has to offer. They might require their children to do their homework before being allowed to choose between playing computer games, texting friends, listening to i-Pods, and whatever else teenagers do to amuse themselves nowadays. The law prohibits certain choices when made by adults—using addictive drugs, drinking while driving, engaging in sex with minors. In general, it is necessary to specify the constraints needed to bring choices more exactly into line with what is deemed to be acceptable behavior.

But what about the costs of imposing and enforcing the constraints? There is a social cost attached to the constraint that requires consumers to pay for an item before they leave the store with it. There are costs, also, of enforcing the laws against the use of addictive drugs, underage drinking, and other forbidden forms of behavior mentioned earlier. Economists do not necessarily take these constraints as a given. There is, in particular, a substantial literature on the question of whether it is socially beneficial, considering the enforcement costs, to prohibit the use of addictive drugs.

On the other hand, there are many constraints on human conduct, the costs of which are either unavoidable or perceived as unavoidable.

The costs incurred in enforcing these constraints are seen as overhead costs, not attributable to a single policy but as the cost of civilization itself. Such costs include the criminal justice system and the military. We might discuss how legalizing drugs would reduce the cost of maintaining the criminal justice system but not how legalizing theft (as in "defund the police") would have the same effect.

What neoclassical economics does is explain how people choose within whatever constraints are imposed by nature, available resources, parents, the law, custom, and other compelling forces and circumstances. Under perfect competition and barring externalities, the choices lead to a social optimum, given the constraints and given individual preferences. Penalties apply to a failure to optimize within the specified constraints. There is scant attention given to the cost of enforcing the constraints themselves.

The question arises, then, of how to model the imposition of constraints on individual choices. Conceptually, politicians could be constrained to choose within the boundaries determined by the constitution, legislative rules, and voter sentiment. The question then is how voter sentiment compares to consumer sentiment.

When a consumer buys a car, he anticipates a certain stream of benefits measured by durability, safety, gas mileage, comfort, and other factors. The consumer then forms a judgment about the car based on his experience with these factors. If he finds that the car won't work, he won't buy it.

But what does it mean for a politician to institute a policy that doesn't work? When politicians pass laws aimed ostensibly at bringing about a certain result, there is usually no way to determine whether the laws brought about the intended result. Consider what happens when the constituent "buys" the passage of a minimum wage law. Much as a consumer must pay for a car, the voter pays for this law through the higher prices he must pay for goods produced by workers affected by the law or, perhaps, by losing his job. Rational behavior on the part of the consumer/voter would require an expectation on his part of certain results, particularly, we can assume, improved worker well-being. This requires a method of measuring worker well-being and then tracking changes in worker well-being attributable to the minimum wage.

The customer can make a rational choice between cars because the car manufacturer and the car dealer have an incentive to provide a car that lives up to the promised standards. The dealer and the manufacturer are constrained to keep the promises they make by the law, by the warranty that the manufacturer must provide to get the customer's business, and by the importance to the manufacturer and dealer to retain the customer's good will. They are constrained also by the fact that the customer will know exactly how well the car lives up to its expectations. No one would buy a car unless the manufacturer and dealer were thus constrained to make good on their promises. Car manufacturers voluntarily constrain themselves with warranties because by doing so they attract customers.

Yet, voters "buy" policies from politicians all the time without anything approaching a similar guarantee. First, the voters, as we saw, vote out of sentiment. Car buyers might buy in part out of sentiment, but they also buy expecting certain observable results. The voter knows that his vote counts for almost nothing except the sentimental reward he gets from casting it, while the car buyer knows that the money he spends on the car results in a meaningful result—he gets the car. Thus, the voter, having sacrificed little to cast a vote that counts for almost nothing, does not impose an expectation on the candidate for office similar to what he imposes on the car manufacturer and dealer when he buys a car. Likewise, the candidate is not constrained and doesn't wish to be constrained to deliver on his promises since the voters will not hold him to them anyway.

If the consumer gets poor service out of the car, the manufacturer suffers immediate and costly penalties. But there is no direct penalty for passing a minimum wage law that performs badly in terms of its ostensible purpose. The result is that the conditions required for compelling rational choice are absent and so, also, is rational choice.

The method by which legislative bodies are able to insulate themselves from the consequences of making irrational choices is to remove choices from their control. If the politician can get voters to accept the imposition of a minimum wage as a cultural necessity, say, on the same order as prohibiting the use of addictive drugs, then the minimum wage becomes a constraint under which they, along with employers and workers, must operate, not a policy to be adopted or rejected.

Consider buzzwords like "fair wage," "living wage," "green jobs," "collective bargaining," and "fair trade." Whenever buzzwords like this are invoked in defense of a policy line, it is because a politician is attempting to immunize himself from the scrutiny that would come with application of the rational choice model. The politician is trying to convert a policy issue into a policy mandate. When a politician makes an appeal to require the payment of a "living wage," he is turning the question of wage determination into a matter of sentiment rather than logic.

The enforcement of the drug laws induces some drug users to break into homes and steal to pay for drugs whose price is inflated by the scarcity of drugs that it is the purpose of the laws to bring about. But if the goal of having a drug-free country trumps personal security, then the cost to homeowners of security systems, locks, guard dogs, and the other preventive measures they might take are built into social policy.

Indeed, if the policy is a drug-free country, then homeowners could be seen as having an obligation to provide sufficient security to deter drugged-out thieves from invading their homes. If they suffer losses for failing to protect their property in the first place, then that is only because they didn't take adequate measures. They should be held accountable for having facilitated the break-in that will permit the drug user to get more drugs.

It is much the same as with homeowners who must put up a fence of certain height to protect children from getting into their swimming pool. The cost of the fence is not a cost with which policy makers feel they must concern themselves with since it is a cost that they make the responsibility of the homeowner.

Politicians who ban indoor smoking do not care whether some people would prefer not to be barred from indoor smoking. The politicians have decided on the basis of sentiment, and very little scientific evidence, that smoking indoors is simply bad.

Sentiment is also the source of claims about "settled science" or "settled social policy." It is in the interest of the politician who brands himself with a certain ideology to speak in terms that presuppose that ideology to be beyond question. "We need to do all we can to promote green energy." Why? Because it is "settled science" that the earth is warming and that the result will be widespread environmental and economic harm.

People making this argument present the scientific argument for global warming as so compelling as to obviate any questioning of its authority or any thought of assessing its economic implications. There is no need to quibble about economics when the rising seas will obliterate our coastal cities in a few generations. And there is no need to quibble about whether the state of California acting alone, or even the entire country acting alone, can do much to reduce CO_2 emissions. We're talking about sentiments here, and sentiments have little to do with logic.

What about "the free market"? It, too, can be, and is, used as a buzzword. The difference is that perfect competition, one instantiation of the free market, provides a framework for the analysis of policies enacted and implemented by politicians, whereas the other buzzwords are intended to appeal to sentiment and to render analysis unnecessary. Buzzwords reflect what is perceived to be common knowledge. Everyone knows that the earth is warming and that we need to do something about it.

Contemporary analogues to this standard are admonitions to choose tap over bottled water or green energy over fossil-fuel energy. Such admonitions are not the result of custom but of efforts by environmentalists to embed them into the belief system of the populace. Thus, the appearance of the modern preacher-equivalent has the effect of shaming miscreants into compliance.

Social standards of this kind are intended to impose constraints on individual choice. What would otherwise be a matter of individual choice then becomes a mandate. The people who embed such mandates into the culture thus do not attempt to repeal rational choice but to render it unnecessary.

The process of embedding the green-energy buzzword into the culture has required assistance from climatologists and physicists. The process of embedding the minimum-wage standard or tax-the-rich standard into the culture consists mainly in creating a presumption of unfairness on the part of anyone who might question the legitimacy of either.

What we must understand, however, is that all such standards exist as a result of the success on the part of their creators at nourishing the proclivity of their audiences to buy into sentiments over rational choice. The rational choice model is seen as unsophisticated and overly limiting. A better model is one in which we think beyond the artificial limitations of rational choice. The case for green energy and fair wages trumps the narrow confines of rational choice.

Creating Memes

There is a name for buzzwords like green energy that become durably implanted in people's minds. That name is "meme." Richard Dawkins has, with the enthusiastic help of Daniel Dennett, popularized the idea of "memes," which are the cultural equivalent of genes and which replicate themselves in a similar fashion. Memes are concepts subject to natural selection that form themselves, as Dennett puts it, into "more or less identifiable cultural units." Such units are "the smallest units that replicate themselves with reliability and fecundity" (Dennett 1991, 201).

Are memes good for us? Dennett insists that "there is no *necessary* connection between a meme's replicative power, its 'fitness' from its point of view, and its contribution to *our* fitness" (Dennett 1991, 203). Yet Dennett is hopeful:

> Although some memes definitely manipulate us into collaborating on their replication *in spite of* our judging them useless or ugly or even dangerous to our health and welfare, many—most if we are lucky—of the memes that replicate themselves do so not just with our blessings but *because of* our esteem for them (Dennett 1991, 203).

Among these good memes are, according to Dennett, "cooperation, music, writing, calendars, education, environmental awareness, arms reduction; and such particular memes as the Prisoner's Dilemma, *The Marriage of Figaro, Moby Dick,* returnable bottles, the SALT agreements" (Dennett 1991, 203). We can't be sure, but it seems that Dennett would have included green energy and fair wages, as well.

Dennett's optimism blends nicely with Wittman's argument that voters keep themselves informed of their representatives' ideology. Voters, Wittman concedes, may be badly informed about their representatives' voting records. But no matter. In Wittman's view, it is not important that voters know how a politician voted on a specific issue but only that the voter have an accurate "impression" of the politician's "policy stance." In other words, it is enough that whatever meme appeals to the voter, the politician is in harmony with it.

Thus, it testifies to voter sovereignty that voters make judgments about a politician based on shared memes rather than any facts they may recall about his voting record. Impressions are good enough if they are based on perceptions that correspond to voting records. Also, research "shows that a significant number of voters are able to identify the positions of candidates on issues and that these positions are good predictors of voting behavior" (Wittman 1995, 11).

Political markets, as Wittman calls them, work efficiently in large measure because they demand so little of the voter.

> It is not necessary to be extremely knowledgeable in order to make correct choices in the political sphere. Consider the standard Downsian model of a left–right continuum of voters' preferences. In order for the voter to make a correct choice, she need only know which candidate is closer to her most desired preference (Wittman 1995, 13).

Thus, a voter, Sally, didn't need to know anything about Joe Biden in order to vote for him except that he came closer than Donald Trump to her liking. By this logic, the idea of "democratic failure" is deemed a "myth."

Contravening Wittman's happy story is the fact that at election time Sally's preferences would have been hopelessly uninformed about such campaign issues as raising marginal tax rates on the "rich," expanding government health care, or running massive deficits to the end of "building back better." Sally would have succeeded only in ratifying the ideology of a presidential candidate intent on further insulating the memes that decided the election—"taxes on the rich," "expanded health care," "reduced global warming"—from exposure to rational thought.

Smith as a Destroyer of the Mercantilist Meme

Consider the mercantilist issue that was a major concern of Adam Smith in *The Wealth of Nations*. Then, as now, mercantilism represented a concrete solution to a problem: imposing trade barriers to expand business for domestic producers. The interests of domestic producers are always immediate and apparent, while the interests of consumers are distant and hypothetical. The collectivist wins over voters by urging concrete solutions over hypothetical market solutions.

Consider how Smith challenged the mercantilist meme. He forced the reader to think in terms of the purpose of economic activity. We work, we invest, we save, not because those activities are ends in themselves but because they are means to the end we seek, namely consumption. Smith's goal was to deny British producers the ability to portray themselves as protectors of the national economy and to reveal them, instead, as special pleaders who used whatever platitudes (memes) they could to advance their interests at the expense of the general public.

Smith's method was to deny British producers a logical justification for their goal of getting Britain to protect them from foreign competition. But the mercantilist could have been understandable to the general public only as long as the general public failed to understand that it is their wants that come first and not those of domestic producers. The purpose of economic activity is to get goods into the hands of consumers with the least amount of effort. If that goal can be accomplished by having the British producer produce wine, then all right. But if British consumers can have more wine for the same amount of effort by exporting cloth and importing wine, then that is all to the better.

The goal of the economist is to induce the people to whom an analysis is presented to reject as untenable the view that the welfare of one interest group trumps that of everyone else. Once mercantilists realize that they can't be seen as advancing the public interest by hanging on to a disproved model, they will abandon that model and accept the inevitability of losing market share to their foreign competitors—or so Smith must have told himself.

Smith presented his model as an alternative to the logically flawed folkish model on which the mercantilists based their argument. But to succeed in this purpose, he had first to get his readers to see through the model the mercantilists were using to make their case (what's good for domestic producers is good for England) and then to see how this model was flawed. The exercise was to draw attention away from the immediately effective solution, that is, tariffs on goods produced abroad, and to focus on the context within which consumers must answer the question of whether to support tariffs. Smith, like Ricardo after him, challenged a popular idea, mercantilism, in terms of its own internal logic, or lack thereof.

One element in the buildup to this challenge was to reinforce the idea that consumers should view the case for mercantilism in terms of their self-interest, just as the mercantilists viewed it in terms of theirs. And a step toward that goal was to establish the role of self-interest as a general motivating principle in human affairs. Unlike animals, said Smith, human beings need the cooperation of others in order to make their way through life. But they cannot hope to get this cooperation by depending on "benevolence only." Man "will be more likely to prevail" if in dealing with others "he can interest "their self-love in his favor." In a famous passage, he summed things up thusly:

It is not from the benevolence of the butcher, the brewer, or the baker, that we expect our dinner but from their regard to their own interest. We address ourselves, not to their humanity but to their self-love, and never talk to them of our necessities but of their advantages (Smith 1976a, 18).

Arthur Jerry Z. Muller writes of the intellectual kinship between Voltaire and Smith. Voltaire, Muller writes, popularized "two important themes: the legitimization on political grounds of the *pursuit* of wealth through economic activity" and "the moral legitimization of the *consumption* of wealth" (Muller 2002, 23). He quotes Voltaire as saying, "It is love of self that encourages love of others, it is through our mutual needs that we are useful to the human race. That is the foundation of all commerce, the eternal link between men." Had God created people "solely concerned with the good of others," then "merchants would have gone to the Indies out of charity and the mason would have cut stone to give pleasure to his neighbor" (Muller 2002, 35).

This emphasis on self-interest became a permanent feature of mainstream economics as it matured from the classical to the neoclassical school. Throughout this process, the appeal to self-interest came from the understanding that self-interested behavior channeled through the marketplace can lead to the greater good.

While enlightenment philosophers such as Smith and Voltaire imbued self-interest with a central role in organizing free markets, others use it to rationalize departures from the free-market model. There are economists who reassure workers that they will get higher wages under the minimum wage without having to worry about losing their jobs.

The argument for a minimum wage presupposes that workers lucky enough not to lose their jobs will use the increased wage to engage in increased consumption. But this benefit depends on the existence of a market economy undistorted by interventions such as the minimum wage. To advocate for a minimum wage is to say something like the following to the workers who are supposed to benefit from its imposition:

> I want you to be confident that you will enjoy higher pay without risking your jobs. You can be confident also that, because the economy is mostly free of distortions such as the very minimum wage from which you will benefit, you will be able to maximize the utility you get from your increased wages. Now let's just be sure that other interest groups don't follow our example and attempt to extract their own favors from government, with the result of reducing the capacity of the market to provide you with the goods the minimum wage is intended to put at your disposal.

The imposition of a minimum wage undermines the argument that no group of special pleaders should permit their self-interest to trump those of everyone else. In that sense, the minimum wage, like other such nostrums, opens channels through which self-interest can operate to the detriment, rather than the benefit, of all. The rhetoric used to sell the minimum wage to the public switches the conversation from one in which workers address their employer according to his self-love to one in which workers address him in terms of their own "necessities."

Stigler, as we saw, could not brook Smith's eagerness to criticize princes for debasing the currency and thus defrauding creditors. For Stigler, this was preaching and therefore a breach of the economist's code of professional behavior.

Stigler had it exactly wrong. Every economist should be required to attend classes in which the subject was Smith's preaching. In one passage Smith said:

> Corporation laws enable the inhabitants of towns to raise their prices, without fearing to be under-sold by the free competition from their own countrymen. Those other regulations secure them equally against that of foreigners. The enhancement of price occasioned by both is every-where finally paid by the landlords, farmers and laborers of the country, who have seldom opposed the establishment of such monopolies. They have seldom neither inclination nor fitness to enter into combinations; and the clamor and sophistry of merchants and manufacturers easily persuade them that the private interest of a part, and of a subordinate part of the society, is the general interest of the whole (Smith 1976a, 142–143).

Note that Smith managed to condemn, for their "sophistry," the merchants and manufacturers who used "corporation laws" to create monopolies for themselves and at the same time condemn the "land-lords, farmers and laborers" who made themselves willing victims of this sophistry. Smith thus performed the role that economists are supposed to perform. He disabused merchants of any pretenses they might harbor that their government-sanctioned monopolies are in the public interest and, at the same time, refused to let townspeople take any comfort in their willingness to cooperate in their own exploitation. He let the towns-people know that they could not be perceived as beneficiaries of some form of altruism on the part of the merchants and manufacturers who were exploiting them.

This brings us to an important element in the psychology of special pleaders. In order to extract the greatest possible satisfaction through the exploitation of their fellow citizens, it is important for the beneficiaries of monopoly power conferred by government to believe that the people they exploit perceive themselves to be beneficiaries, not victims. Thus, the actual beneficiaries of this monopoly power can indulge their self-love by simultaneously benefiting directly from the favors conferred on them by government and believing that they are perceived to be benefactors rather than exploiters.

The economist faces a challenge here because, in exposing a monopoly for what it is, he also threatens the self-regard of all those people who previously thought themselves to be beneficiaries rather than victims. People do not like to question their ideologies even when it can be shown that their ideologies conflict with their own interests. People need to see the world in some consistent manner, rather than as a jumble of conflicting realities. Seeing that you have bought gullibly into some ideology that is now shown to violate your personal interest is a painful matter.

Here again, the neoclassical model becomes a necessary tool in the arsenal of economic persuasion. The only effective way of exposing for what it is the sophistry that makes government-sponsored monopolies politically viable is to confront belief with logic. The manufacturer licensed by local government to keep out competition can no longer feel confident in his ability to perpetuate the comfort that others have taken in this arrangement. Even if the consumers victimized by this exploitation don't fully comprehend what has been going on, the manufacturer must worry that the jig is up and the protection he enjoyed may soon vanish.

The power of the neoclassical model in this setting derives, again, from the fact that it is internally consistent and that it punctures the myth that monopoly is good for everyone. Granted, the model presupposes rational choice, sorely lacking so far on the part of those consumers who have gullibly acquiesced in their own exploitation. But that doesn't matter. People want to believe that they think rationally and to be seen as thinking rationally. They need to be goaded into thinking rationally, however much they wish to sit comfortably within their own world view. And the only way to goad them into doing so is to appeal to them in terms of their own rationality, however much wishful thinking that might entail.

In this regard, it is important to keep in mind the fact that, while neoclassical economics presupposes rationality, the neoclassical economist need not. He need only figure that people will not see themselves as willingly sacrificing something they want when that something is available to them at no additional cost. Once a British consumer sees that he can have more wine than before without sacrificing any cloth, the choice is clear. It is not that this consumer has been rational all along, happily maximizing utility, but that, when confronted by the stark choice between more and less, rationality will kick in and he will choose more.

People may nod their heads when told how irrational they are. Yes, they drink and some still smoke despite the known harmful effects of both. But they will not accept abstract arguments predicated on their irrationality. The rational choice assumption is the instrument, and rationality is the goal.

The task facing the economist becomes more difficult, the more difficult it is to frame the available choices. The economist wants to frame choices as, for example: "Would you prefer more wine to less, were the government to lift trade barriers on wine?" "Would you prefer to be free to work for this employer at any wage on which you agree, or would you prefer for government to tell your employer the wage that he must pay if he is to hire you?"

These are rhetorical questions, asked to provoke the person to whom they are addressed into seeing the choice before him in a rational light. But because politicians don't want to be judged according to criteria rationally arrived at, they do their best to avoid such questions. They want the questions to be posed in such a way that there is no single yes or no answer.

An example of such a question might be: "Do you think that people should be able to get faster access to their doctors and to get more of their doctor's time than they can now?" That question is not so simple. It can't be answered without getting answers to a lot of other questions first. Does the government propose to encourage entry into the medical profession? To do that, will it raise reimbursements for care provided to Medicare and Medicaid patients? Well, that would require higher taxes and the higher taxes may not be worth the benefits. Should we eliminate the tax deductibility of health care premiums? That would reduce the demand for doctor's services, thus freeing up doctors to give more time to their patients. But that raises other, equally daunting questions about whether we really want to put an end to the subsidization of health care.

The government insulates itself from accountability by making policies so complex as to defy the consideration of meaningful choices and answers to yes-or-no questions. It is easier to avoid hard questions if it is impossible for people affected by a policy to figure out what questions to ask.

The role of neoclassical economics is to put questions before people that motivate clear choices between the options available to them. In performing this role, economists will encounter the objection that "the choice is not so simple." The answer to this objection is that the issue has been made deliberately complex in order to avoid the necessity of providing an answer. Complexity is a device used by the beneficiaries of government policies to prevent simple choices from being offered to the people who pay, in one way or another, for those choices.

The marketplace serves to encourage rational choice by putting hard choices before people engaged in market activities. The shopper in the supermarket may find it difficult to choose because so many choices are set before her. Yet, she will choose because the family needs to eat and because there is only so much money in the food budget.

The shopper in the market for policies and politicians is under no such constraint. She has no government budget akin to her food budget to allocate between roads and schools or between defense and environmental protection. Were she to think for a minute that she must be compelled to choose between these options in the same manner as she must choose between steak and hamburger, there are lobbyists posing as economists who will rush to say that she need not feel at all so constrained. It is not between roads and schools that she must choose but between "essential" government services and a few cups of coffee a month, between "investments" that require a small sacrifice now but that will pay off handsomely later. No need to choose between roads and schools at all when the cost, such as it is, of having both is so modest.

The marketplace poses a threat to collectivism because it encourages the idea that, given clear choices, made under tight constraints, people will choose rationally. The economist must say to the voter, "Here are the measured benefits of proposed increases in spending on roads and schools. Here are the costs. Decide whether the spending is in your interest or not."

Politicians do not want policy questions to be presented in such terms. They want the questions to be about sentiment rather than logic. It is thus that they are able to perpetuate spending policies for which there is no explicit rational justification. This is in contrast to the marketplace, where the absence of any rational justification for a particular action or practice usually spells its doom. Wherever rational choice is not suppressed by the contrivance of politicians and wherever there are penalties for not choosing rationally, people choose rationally. This, they will often do, at the expense of culture and existing institutions.

The Saga of Justus Möser

Jerry Z. Muller discusses the thoughts of Justus Möser, an 18th-century administrator of the town of Osnabrück, Germany, who blamed the erosion of local culture on the emergence of the marketplace. Trade required uniformity in laws and standards across regions and nations, and Möser resisted the subordination of local laws and standards to this necessity. The pressure for standardization threatened the local culture, which Möser saw as deserving to survive despite the obstacles that it created to free trade across national and local boundaries.

It is important to recognize that, in important respects, Möser was a predecessor to Edmund Burke, Friedrich Hayek, and other historically important commentators on the importance of culture. Möser objected to what Hayek later came to see as the "scientistic" nature of Enlightenment thinking—the idea that man can order social institutions by the pure force of reason, stripped of historical and cultural context. Möser "contrasted the claims of rationalist theory with the deeper rationality of local, historical experience," an idea that presaged arguments to be made centuries later by Hayek and Thomas Sowell about the richness of institutions and cultures that the intellectuals of their time, in their "liberal conceit," would sweep away for the purpose of imposing top-down, rationalistic solutions (Muller 2002, 88).

The intellectual appeared in Möser's work in variety of guises, all negative. In one guise, the intellectual was "rich in Latin learning but poor in the experience of the world." In another,

> he was the learned fool, like the sacristan who proclaimed grand ideas for economic development based on foreign models and who dismissed the wisdom of the past as "prejudice," but whose wisdom of the world was so scanty that he barely knew how to set the church sundial (Muller 2002, 88).

Möser condemned government for reasons opposite of today's conservatives. The economic ordinances of central government that were proclaimed in order to facilitate trade were, for Möser, "destructive of private property and violations of freedom" (Muller 2002, 86). The market economy was destroying "civic virtue." Muller quotes Möser as saying: "Money and paid service … have shamefully extinguished the economy of public honor which were the nonmonetary means by which patriots were honored" (Muller 2002, 102).

A major criticism of the free-market model lies in this notion that it creates a soulless class of money-seekers who are loyal only to themselves and who run roughshod over long-beloved traditions that get in the way of personal gain. It is a criticism that we can trace back to Aristotle and that is not without merit. The thought here, though, is that capitalism will triumph unless stopped in its tracks and that government is alone among institutions with the wherewithal to stop it in its tracks. (*Personal note*: I discovered a few weeks ago that Sirius/XM radio had replaced the Metropolitan Opera channel with, of all things, the Elvis Channel. This was not the fault of government, but it fits Möser's narrative.)

It happens that, in Möser's time, government was in the business of removing, rather than imposing, obstacles to commerce. Thus, for example, the government had previously supported the guilds in their refusal to admit children of low social standing or born out of wedlock. When the Hapsburgs repealed this policy, employers were happy to accept the benefits of the increased supply of labor. But Möser was appalled at the result and said so in an essay entitled "On the Diminished Shame of Whores and Children in Our Day" (Muller 2002, 92).

The exclusionary practices of the guilds, which limited access to socially favored individuals, could not stand up to the market economy once government switched from enforcing to forbidding those practices. The rulers of that time made up their minds to get out of the way of the burgeoning market economy and to take with them such barriers to free markets as they had previously sanctioned.

Thus it is that economic freedom lives or dies according to the whims of Leviathan. In 18th-century Germany, government opened up job opportunities for people previously denied those opportunities. Today, government sets minimum wages for unskilled jobs. Through the prevailing wage law, it also sets wages on public construction jobs at above-market levels and through Project Labor Agreements attempts to limit access to those jobs to union workers.

In 18th-century Germany, government aimed to break down class distinctions that barred people from work. Now government rewards a class of politically favored workers who belong to construction unions at the expense of the 86 percent of workers who do not.

Why were the Hapsburgs of 18th-century Germany unwilling to enforce a labor monopoly against the rising tide of capitalism whereas the president of 21st-century America is eager to shore up the wage premium earned by a declining coterie of union construction workers? The answer lies in how politicians that benefit from union support have, with the help of the unions themselves, been able to manipulate the choices that voters see themselves as having over this matter. The guilds of Möser's day did not enjoy that kind of clout.

An 18th-century carriage manufacturer operating out of Osnabrück had no difficulty communicating to the local rulers the choice he would make between costly labor and less costly labor, given the opportunity to choose between the two. And the rulers decided that they would risk the debasement of public morality if doing so made it possible for the carriage manufacturer to hire more workers and produce more carriages. Such was the mindset of that time.

Muller begins his essay on Möser with the subtitle "The Market as a Destroyer of Culture." Voltaire saw the market's destructive effects on culture in a positive light: The market breaks down cultural barriers to religious toleration. Möser, as we have seen, saw it in a negative light. Both understood that there is a conflict between market and culture, against which culture stands little chance. Culture is not in and of itself the creature of government. The Hapsburgs had to remove the laws that made it possible for the guilds to enforce their exclusionary policies but the practices themselves—the policies of excluding people of low station and birth—were cultural in origin.

The reason for the weak position commanded by culture in this battle is that capitalism puts choices before people in such a way as to compel a choice between culture and material gain. The fact that causes so much anguish is that the guardians of culture—the clerics, the knights, the intellectuals, the local conservation commission—find themselves in an uneven contest when pitted against the forces of capitalism. In that battle, capitalism is the face of modernity, against which there is no defense.

When Christian objections to usury stood in the way of providing financial capital to business during the Middle Ages, Jews, who had no such proscriptions, stepped in to fill the void. And eventually Christianity came to accommodate itself to this sin. Thus also, those of us who don't like big box stores have had to accommodate ourselves to the sight of our local appliance and hardware stores losing out to Walmart and Home Depot.

Möser stands near the beginning of a centuries-old debate over the value of protecting culture against the inroads of capitalism. And, absurd though his arguments generally were, he had a point. "Change" is never in and of itself a good thing. There is no presumption that societal upheavals brought about by a spread of market activity works to the advantage of mankind, just as there is no presumption in favor of laws that inhibit the spread of market activity. The difference has to do with power. When it comes to culture, its guardians, unaided by the power of government or threats of violence, can do little to stop the capitalist juggernaut. Likewise, the guardians of capitalism, who consist mainly of a few intellectuals hidden away in academic departments, can do little to stop the advance of collectivism.

It is an odd feature of modern life that capitalism now runs amuck in Communist China while socialism is showing new life in America. Why this turn of events? Because the Communists swept away the cultural barriers to economic development and then, with the failure of central planning, left a void that capitalism came to fill. On the other hand, the defenders of capitalism in the United States have become flaccid in their efforts to stem the tide.

Burke and Culture

The British parliamentarian Edmund Burke wrote at a time when capitalism was on the rise. Like Möser, he understood the threat to culture posed by the 18th-century Enlightenment, of which he was a part. Unlike Möser, he wrote approvingly of the advance of capitalism. He opposed the minimum wage.

Burke did argue for the preservation of culture as necessary for making life worth living. But he believed that commerce need not be the enemy of culture, but rather its natural offspring. Only when the "monied interests" threaten to undermine the very institutions that permit them to pursue money does a conflict arise.

Burke was a passionate defender of the culture of his time. The capacity of the monied interests to threaten their own livelihood was manifest by their opportunistic alliance with "political men of letters," whose purpose it was to sweep away religion and all other remnants of the past.

Muller writes of how Burke "ridiculed the propensity of some enlightened intellectuals to judge institutions by abstract principles" and of how Burke "insisted that the attempt to do so would delegitimate all existing institutions without being able to create better ones in their place" (Muller 2002, 130). "For Burke, almost everything that makes life worthwhile is a result of society, its inherited codes, knowledge and institutions. These goods are fragile and when they are destroyed, the result is human misery" (Muller 2002, 131).

And it was the French Revolution that became for Burke the worst-case scenario for the destruction of those fragile goods. It was, said Burke, the "men of letters"—the Nihilists of his day—who had, as Möser puts it, "delegitimated the monarchy, the aristocracy, and the taxing powers of the state in the eyes of the larger public" (Muller 2002, 130). The result was the murderous binge of which that larger public partook and that caused the streets of Paris to run red with blood.

Culture, defined as Western values, needs its defenders because the consequence of its erosion is the French Revolution, Aushwitz, the Gulag, and now the streets of Portland, Oregon. Burke was right in pointing out that Western culture must be protected if capitalism is to survive. Indeed, if mainstream economics is to survive, so must the cultural foundations of capitalism.

We cannot look to the Austrians and Randians for help since they have become instruments for the destruction of the very system that they purport to champion. Theirs is a fantasy world in which the glue that holds capitalism together is a by-product of the very capitalism for which it is a prerequisite. Man, we learn from these quarters, can create his own moral order merely by understanding the importance of self-love and of trust in the conduct of economic affairs. Trust need not be enforced by laws or courts because everyone engaging in commerce will understand its importance and honor spontaneously the trust put in them by creditors and customers.

Unfortunately, Burke did not foresee how he was providing intellectual ammunition for the Austrians and Randians, whose ideas would eventually degenerate into nihilism. His famous lamentation over the death of chivalry and the triumph of "oeconomists" and "calculators" is easily seen as, and was probably intended to be, a rebuke to the emerging science of economics. But, contrary to what Burke implied, it is not overconfidence in "reason" that threatens to undermine the cultural prerequisites for capitalism but the failure to apply reason that creates an ever-growing legal and cultural barrier to capitalism. We are not sliding into collectivism only because of the hubris of intellectuals who think that they can plan a top-down economic system. We are sliding into socialism because people are willing to accept nonrational justifications for the collectivist agenda.

It is true, as Möser warned, that the contest between culture and capitalism is an uneven one. Actually, that can be a very good thing. If capitalism someday puts an end to clitoral mutilation and the practice of punishing young girls for attending school, then three cheers for capitalism. But the tension between markets and culture is a general one and needs to be addressed.

Economists are akin to soldiers whose job it is to clear out enemy troops while avoiding harm to noncombatants. Like soldiers, they will inevitably inflict collateral damage. They will inadvertently clear away collectivist policies that had the effect of doing some good. Of this, they need not and cannot be concerned. We cannot let Möser's or Burke's concerns about the triumph of reason over culture obscure the fact that it is only through reason that we can turn back the collectivist tide.

What economists must do is remain conscious of the institutional and cultural foundations that make capitalism possible and, with it, their own jobs. They must not let the free-market model be hijacked in the service of boutique theories that extol anarchy or that romanticize capitalist giants who will lead us to the mountain top.

CHAPTER 7

Economics and Cognitive Science

In Chapter 2, we saw that the job of the economist doesn't end with revealing economic truth. For the truth to matter, it is also necessary for the people to whom the economist directs his appeal to act on what they learn. But that means delving into the thought processes of the economist's audience. As already seen, writers in the philosophy of economics have been exploring the nexus between economics and the mind. This development has come about in large part because of the growing importance since World War II of cognitive science, the purpose of which is to explain how the mind works.

Cognitive science has been around since Plato. But the idea that the study of how the mind works is not just philosophy, but also "science" did not take hold until the mechanical computer came along and with it the notion that mechanical computation resembles or perhaps operates in a fashion identical to the mind.

The Turing Machine

In a 1950 article, Alan Turing, who had earlier conceptualized the "Turing machine," as a hypothetical computer, raised the question, "Can machines think?" His answer was that the question was "too meaningless to deserve discussion." Nevertheless, he believed that "at the end of the century, the use of the words and general educated opinion will have altered so much that one will be able to speak of machines thinking without expecting to be contradicted" (Turing 1950, 442).

Turing changed his question from whether machines can think to whether a machine could provide answers to a series of questions in such a way as to make it impossible for a human observer to tell whether the answers were provided by a machine or a human. Turing argued that once machine computation had become indistinguishable from human think-ing, computers could be deemed thinking machines (Turing 1950, 442). Perhaps the first foray by an economist into this territory came when, in his *Sensory Order*, Friedrich Hayek compared the human mind to "certain statistical machines for sorting cards on which punched holes represent statistical data" (Hayek 1976, 49).

The question of how people think became important to economics once it became clear that purely objective theories of value, based on "real" labor costs, were unworkable. Economics had to develop its own theory of how people think in order to provide a theory of value that had the requisite generality.

As described, the advent of the neoclassical school of economics in the late 19th century signaled a shift from a theory of value based on labor cost to one based on individual subjective preferences. In neoclassi-cal economics, economic agents, usually defined to be individual decision makers (but also sometimes firms or nations), make choices in such a way as to maximize utility—an entirely subjective concept.

Behaviorism and Its Architects

Adam Smith foreshadowed behavioral economics when he wrote of man's "propensity to truck, barter, and exchange one thing for another" (Smith 1976a, 17). One might say that behaviorism skips the question of what determines value or how value springs out of the minds of economic agents and simply asks what agents do when stim-ulated by hunger, advertising, sexual attraction, or other such external phenomena.

Behaviorism rejects the idea of rational choice. It is possible to observe but not to explain choice. Methodological behaviorism, Searle claims, has morphed into "logical behaviorism," whereby there were no mental states as such but only dispositions toward certain kinds of behavior. Consider the belief that it is going to rain. Searle explained methodological behav-iorism as claiming that such a belief has meaning only in terms of the rain avoidance behavior that it stimulates. It is not, as Searle puts it, that

Jones "believes that it is going to rain" but that he was disposed to close the windows or carry an umbrella (Searle 2004, 36). There are no mental states to consider but only actions to be observed.

A subsequent development was the emergence of "identity theory," whereby mental states are reducible to brain states. Whatever sensations you might have at this moment, they are just states of the brain and nothing more. The mental is really just the physical.

Yet another approach is to invoke "functionalism," whereby "mental states ... are defined as states that have certain sorts of functions, and the notion of a function is explained in terms of causal relations to external stimuli, to other mental states, and to external behavior" (Searle 2004, 43). Mental states are not defined by what is in the mind but by what kind of behavior they motivate. "A belief is just an entity that, standing in certain relationships to input stimuli to other mental states, will cause external behavior" (Searle 2004, 44).

Another view explored by Searle is the "connection principle," whereby we describe "a brain mechanism, not in terms of its neural biological properties, but in terms of its capacity to cause conscious states and behavior" (Searle 2004, 171).

Finally, we can consider eliminativism, according to which, as Searle describes it, "mental states do not exist at all." Eliminativism associates the existence of mental states with "folk psychology," which is to say ordinary beliefs, desires, and intentions (Searle 2004, 52–53).

In a seminal article, Paul M. Churchland defined eliminativism as:

> the thesis that our common-sense conception of psychological phenomena constitutes a radically false theory, a theory so fundamentally defective that both the principles and the ontology of that theory will eventually be displaced, rather than smoothly reduced, by completed neuroscience. Our mutual understanding and even our introspection may then be reconstituted within the conceptual framework of completed neuroscience, a theory we may expect to be more powerful by far than the common-sense psychology it displaces, and more substantially integrated within physical science generally (Churchland 1981, 67).

For Churchland, "one's *introspective* certainty that one's mind is the seat of beliefs and desires may be as badly misplaced as was the classical man's *visual* certainty that the star-flecked sphere of the heavens turns daily" (Churchland 1981, 70). To believe that our minds possess some form of intentionality is akin to the belief in primitive cultures that "the wind could know anger, the moon jealousy, the river generosity, the sea fury, and so forth" (Churchland 1981, 74).

Thus also Don Ross informs us that "contemporary cognitive science is not sympathetic to the idea that arcane principles of formal rational choice, any more than the refined discoveries of economic analysis in general, are to be determined by continued and careful introspection" (Ross 2005a, 92).

As we have seen, a philosopher important to Ross's view of economics is Daniel Dennett. Dennett turns Churchland's criticism of folk psychology on its head by redefining the purpose of intentionality. The purpose is not to reflect someone's mental state but to predict his behavior. Dennett's thesis is:

> that while belief is a perfectly objective phenomenon … it can be discerned only from the point of view of one who adopts a certain *predictive strategy*, and its existence can be confirmed only by an assessment of the success of that strategy (Dennett 1989, 15).

An intentional strategy "consists of treating the object whose behavior you want to predict as a rational agent with beliefs and desires and other mental stages exhibiting … *intentionality*" (Dennett 1989, 15). We predict behavior according to what we know about the person's (the object's) beliefs and desires and about how the person will go about achieving its desires. Thus, if we take the intentional stance toward an object that has a desire to win at chess and predict correctly that it tries to win at chess, a chess-playing computer becomes ontologically equivalent to a chess-playing man.

"The deeper pressure I mean to apply against mature anthropocentric neoclassicism," says Ross, "is based on its commitment to the idea that a given biological person must be a *single* agent across her whole temporal biography" (Ross 2005a, 155). "As a matter of logic," he says, "an *economic agent* must have stable preferences; otherwise RPT [revealed preference theory][1] does not apply to it" (Ross 2005a, 157).

"In trying to understand human behavior, one of the things we need to do is model people as marketplaces of subpersonal interests (and as themselves embedded in social marketplaces). These subpersonal interests are *just* utility functions" (Ross 2005a, 355).

Rational Thought, After All

These challenges aside, it is still possible to find support for rational choice in the cognitive science literature. Andy Clark writes about a "mangrove effect," which relates to a particular chicken-and-egg problem. Consider a tree growing on a desert island. Which came first, the island or the tree? You say, "The island, of course." "Not so fast," says Clark. Consider the mangrove tree, which roots in a mud flat below the water in which its seed floats. The tree is formed as its seedling sends roots down to the mud flat below, and the resulting root system traps floating debris, which then forms itself into a small island around the tree. More seedlings lead to more trees and more islands that may eventually merge into one large island. You might think that the island came first, but it was actually the trees (Clark 1998, 207–208).

"Something like the 'mangrove effect,'" he says, "is operative in some species of human thought." While "it is natural to suppose the words are always rooted in the fertile soil of preexisting thoughts … sometimes, at least, the influence runs in the other direction." Clark, then introduces the term "second-hand cognitive dynamics," by which he means "a cluster of powerful capacities involving self-evaluation, self-criticism, and finely honed remedial responses" that:

> would include recognizing a flaw in our own plan of argument and dedicating further cognitive efforts (i.e., thought) to fixing

---

[1] Revealed Preference Theory maintains that it is possible to derive a consumer demand curve by making just two assumptions about consumer choice: (1) that if I choose A over B now I will always choose A over B as long as I can afford both and (2) if I choose A over B and B over C, I will choose A over C. This formulation omits any consideration of utility and thus avoids the criticism that utility is unobservable.

it, reflecting on the unreliability of our own initial judgments in certain types of situations and proceeding with special caution as a result, coming to see why we reached a particular conclusion by appreciating the logical transitions in our own thought, and thinking about the conditions under which we think best and trying to bring them about (Clark 1998, 208–209).

It is just such self-criticism that this book aims to instantiate in voters and politicians.

The role of neoclassical economics is to cause people "to reflect on the unreliability" of their "own initial judgments" and also to question whether their beliefs are favorably perceived.

Clark correctly points out that "advanced cognition depends crucially on our abilities to *dissipate* reasoning—to diffuse achieved knowledge and practical wisdom through complex social structures and processes" (Clark 1998, 180). Clark emphasizes the importance of "scaffolding" in explaining the ability of people to choose rationally. Scaffolding consists of social constraints that prevent people from thinking irrationally.

According to Clark, "the paradigm of substantive rationality … seems to work best in the highly scaffolded case and to falter and fail as the role of weakly constrained individual cognition increases." So we have a paradox: "Neoclassical economics works best in situations in which individual rational choice has been severely limited by the quasi-evolutionary selection of constraining policies and institutional practices" (Clark 1998, 182). Choices come out better when there is plenty of "scaffolding" to prop them up.

The conception of human rational agency in terms of maximizing over a complete and consistent set of preference orderings is not psychologically realistic. The assumption that the neoclassical firm acts to maximize profits does not apply to the firm by virtue of its internal beliefs and desires. Rather, an environment of competitive capital markets acts as a selector on firms. The firm's interests may arise from features of its environment and need not arise from any particular psychological facts about its members.

In making this argument, Clark cites Satz and Ferejohn, who say:

We believe that rational-choice explanations are most plausible in settings in which individual action is severely constrained, and thus where the theory gets its explanatory power from structure-generated interests and not from actual individual psychology. In the absence of strong environmental constraints, we believe that rational choice is a weak theory, with limited predictive power (Satz and Ferejohn 1994, 72).

Satz and Ferejohn draw a contrast between "voting behavior" and "party behavior" to illustrate their point:

Compare the theory of voting behavior and the theory of party behavior within the theory of electoral competition. In the theory of party behavior, the results are obtained in a purely deductive and theoretical manner. Within plurality-rule systems with two electorally motivated parties, the classical theory of electoral competition makes strong predictions as to what the parties will do in equilibrium. Moreover, within such systems competition among parties for valuable offices encourages them to be relatively electorally motivated, since nonelectoralist parties will tend to remain out of office and be unable to reward their supporters. In this sense, the competitive environment encourages the adoption of electoralist objectives (Satz and Ferejohn 1994, 79).

Similarly, "the competitive environment of capital markets ensures that, by and large, only firms that maximize profits survive" (Clark 1998, p. 182).

On the other hand,

the theory of consumer behavior is weak and less successful. This is because individual worldviews loom large in consumer behavior and the external scaffolding is commensurately weaker. Similarly, the theory of voting behavior is weak in comparison with the theory of party behavior in electoral competitions (Clark 1998, 183).

So, according to Clark and Satz and Ferejohn, external scaffolding imposes constraints that vindicate the neoclassical model under the circumstances described: the firm in competition with other firms and the candidate for office in competition with other candidates. But the neoclassical model is perforce not as reliable when the same scaffolding and constraints are not available. Voters, who see only a weak link between their choices and the consequences of those choices, are less likely to choose rationally. The same goes for consumers.

So we are left with the "unscaffolded" consumers and voters. Economists can have little concern for consumers, and that's because irrational behavior on the part of consumers imposes its own penalties. If I bet the house payment on a roll of the dice at Boston's Encore Casino and lose, that will be self-correcting in its own way. So what's left is voter choice, which should be the prime focus of economists.

The challenge is to get voters to perceive that if they make an irrational choice they will pay a penalty. Again, it is not necessary that they actually do pay a penalty but only that they believe they will.

Nudging Versus Prodding

This turns on its head the idea that the role of economics is to "nudge" people into making good choices, while they remain unmindful of why their choices are bad (Thaler and Sunstein 2008). The objections to this "nudge" approach is that the nudgers can just as well exploit people, as they can protect them from making bad choices.

It is true that market and electoral constraints impose a discipline on businesses and political parties that do not constrain consumers and individual voters. Thus, consumers—individual economic agents, actually—avoid the immediate, adverse consequences of making bad choices and are thus more inclined to make bad choices than are firms constrained by capital markets. Likewise, voters care only remotely whether they are voting for the candidate who best represents their interests and values whereas an election means either winning or losing for the candidates.

Thus, the legislature that votes on a minimum wage law is not constrained in the same fashion as is the employer on whom the minimum wage is imposed. If the legislature makes the "wrong" decision, it incurs no penalty for making that decision in the same way that a firm incurs a penalty for hiring a worker who costs more than he adds to the firm's revenue. Politicians live in a world of perceptions about reality, not reality itself. Even when they stand for election, it is perceptions that drive the win-or-lose result.

Suppose, as has indeed happened, that the U.S. minimum wage aggravates the unemployment problem among teenagers. No politician who voted for the minimum wage will admit that his vote was a mistake. He'll say that the teen unemployment problem is the result of a weak economy and the lack of summer youth projects. The politician is safely ensconced in his mangrove swamp of rationalizations unless he detects that his rationalizations are no longer perceived—shall I say it?—to hold water.

The distinction between the constraints, such as they are, that face the politician in this setting and the constraints that face the employer, on which the politician imposes a further constraint in the form of a minimum wage, is important for the task of exposing the politician's fecklessness. In his analysis of the minimum wage, the economist can correctly assume that employers operate rationally when they see that they have to pay more for labor. Because the employer is scaffolded or constrained in the manner described by Clark and company, the rational choice model does apply. The rational choice model serves as an instrument for predicting the employer's response to the minimum wage.

Legislators vote on the basis of how their votes are perceived by the electorate and by their fellow legislators, not so much on the basis of what substantive effects their votes will have. Yet here the rational choice model is just as apposite as it is in analyzing the employer response to the minimum wage, though for a different reason. It is an instrument but a different sort of instrument. It serves the purpose of challenging the basis on which legislators support or oppose a particular policy.

It is important to distinguish the role of rational choice as an instrument for predicting behavior from its role as an instrument in motivating behavior. In the first role, it operates as an analytical tool. In the second, it operates as a tool aimed at getting people to make the choices they would make if they were rational—at prodding them to choose rationally. The voter supports the minimum wage out of a sentiment that he wishes to help labor, persuaded as he is by the politician who claims to be "pro-labor" and who offers the minimum wage as a palliative. Rational political choice, however, requires the politician to be held accountable for his promise to help labor by imposing the minimum wage. The economist uses the neoclassical model as an instrument for identifying whether the minimum wage does in fact help labor and for goading the voter into making the politician accountable if it doesn't.

The economist bases his analysis of the minimum wage, then, on two necessities: (1) He needs to predict as accurately as possible what effects the minimum wage will have under the assumed conditions, and (2) he needs to present an analysis for comparison against the stated positions on which legislators vote for or against the minimum wage. Inasmuch as legislators don't want to be perceived as predicating their votes on the assumed irrationality of the electorate, it is politically necessary to construct the analysis within a framework that takes it as rational to demand accountability from the legislators who impose the minimum wage. In this fashion only can he hope to lead voters out of the policy swamp.

The current law, as it relates to the minimum wage, taxes, and every other economic issue, is its own mangrove swamp of accumulated complexity. Politicians see it as in their interest to keep this swamp as fertile and impenetrable as possible. The successful politician insulates his positions on the issues from criticism by predicating them on the preservation of a status quo deemed too complex to challenge. Thus, we can't repeal the minimum wage because some of the workers who would be harmed by its repeal are illegal immigrants who can't avail themselves of the earned income tax credit. We can't modify the federal tax code because it is so wrought with complexity that any modification might reward the wealthy. We can't have free trade because of job guarantees made to the wine or cloth makers.

By thus creating as many difficulties as possible that might arise in correcting a wrongheaded policy, the politician makes it easier to resist change. He thus also makes it more difficult to change how he is perceived to be acting. No matter how illogical a law might be, the politician can safely support the law if he can enmesh it in a lattice-work of connections with other laws whose effects might be worsened by its repeal or modification.

Clark and others imply that the decision maker does not conform to the neoclassical model except where forced by external constraints to do so. My argument is that the decision maker faces constraints that have been engineered by politicians to make rational choice difficult.

Politicians pass new laws to correct difficulties created by old laws but then also pass new laws to create further difficulties requiring still newer laws to correct them. The job of the economist is to unravel this web, to focus attention on individual issues (impose the minimum wage or not), and cause legislators to worry that their stated reasons for taking whatever side they take on those issues are untenable.

Politicians encourage irrationality on the part of the voter in order to tighten their hold on their offices. A politician will encourage his constituents to attach what amounts to a high discount rate to any harm they may suffer as a consequence of a tax increase. Or exploit a voter's tendency to resist a change in law that he would never support if newly proposed. Or make laws complex in order to prevent their repeal. Politicians strengthen their grip on the voters by framing issues in a way that causes voters to support the politicians' agenda. The job of the economist is to show that the consequences of the policy are the same, however it is framed.

Whereas classical economics was as much about moral science as it was about science, neoclassical economics is all about science. As discussed in Chapter 4, the economic scientists who led the neoclassical revolution found it necessary to divorce economics from both moral science and the labor theory of value.

According to Robbins, "It may indeed be urged that the more that purposive action becomes conscious of itself, the more it necessarily becomes consistent" (Robbins 1932, 93). Ross claims that "this sentiment is deeply at odds with contemporary cognitive and behavioral science—not to mention ethological facts" (Ross 2005a, 95). Put that way, however, it was Robbins who understood how people think and not Ross.

CHAPTER 8

What Economists Should Do

Economists sometimes help people make business decisions, much as architects help people make choices about the design of a building. And, indeed, some economists function mainly as business advisors.

The economist, qua business advisor, approaches his task with the sense that the law and the marketplace are fixed points in his analysis—beyond his control and representing factors that he must take into account in developing strategies for his clients. The economist who operates in the public policy arena faces a much different problem. For him, the law and the marketplace are not fixed points but variables that his advice might well be intended to influence.

An expert on labor policy might, for example, take on the task of estimating how a proposed minimum wage law would affect employment. He understands that his estimate will bear on the decision whether to support the imposition of a minimum wage,

He would know, going into this job, that there is a sizeable literature on the minimum wage and that economists have already done much research aimed at showing whether, as the neoclassical model predicts, minimum wage laws will cause a loss in jobs. If he works in an environment free of ideological pressure, the economist will then consult this literature and make his own efforts to provide an honest answer, using an econometric model in order to estimate the effects on employment.

What every economist familiar with this issue knows, however, is that it is almost impossible to approach the minimum wage with an absolutely clean slate concerning how he views the issue. First, much research on this topic comes from economists who have been hired by a client who already takes a strong stand, for or against. Frequently, the client knows what the economist he hires is going to say before hiring him. The economist working for a labor union will conclude that the minimum wage has little or no adverse effect on employment. The economist working for a retail association will conclude just the opposite. Even economists working in the ivory tower striving merely to publish in the best journals will approach the task with their own predispositions.

This is to be expected, in view of the inexactness of economics as a science and in view, also, of human nature. Climate scientists and biologists approach their jobs with their own predispositions. It is impossible, anyway, to approach any field of study without some ideological or methodological framework within which to proceed. And the policy maker can very well use the known ideological biases of the economic advisor to look for clues for any flaws in the analysis. An analysis offered by a fierce proponent or opponent of the minimum wage can be valid irrespective of the analyst's personal views, but it is smart to consider how his views might have affected his objectivity.

There is a fundamental difference, also, between the incentives under which public policy economists and business economists do their work. How the business economist fares professionally depends on the quality of the advice he offers, as measured by the success his client enjoys in following it.

In the public sector, however, it is rare for a decision maker to consult an economist for guidance in arriving at a position on some issue and do so with an open mind. It is more common for the economist to be expected to offer a patina of scientific respectability to a position that has already been taken. The job therefore is not to give advice that solves some policy problem but to provide ammunition that permits the client to advance a policy agenda that was decided upon before the economist was consulted. Thus, the economist functions more as a political subaltern than as a social scientist.

The only penalty the economist has to fear is one that might result because his prediction was not persuasive enough to win the day for his client the policy maker. We know one reason why economists are off the hook even when it appears that their policy advice was misbegotten. The reason is that unanticipated economic developments are not easily traced to bad economic advice given by a particular person, at least not in the way that a dead patient or collapsed bridge is traceable to a particular doctor or engineer.

Economists hired to advance a political cause therefore have little reason to build accountability into their advice when they can find gainful employment without bothering to do so and when their clients would not appreciate their efforts. This is quite different from the accountability that a patient expects of his doctor or a public entity expects of its engineers. The result is that economists end up functioning in effect as public relations operatives armed with Excel spreadsheets, putting a happy face on whatever cause it is that they are hired to advance.

Engineers and doctors are disciplined by the importance of their being perceived as competent practitioners of their crafts as measured by client satisfaction. Economists escape this discipline to the extent that client satisfaction has little to do with the accuracy of their work. All that is needed is that the economist has followed existing protocols regarding theoretical rigor. For the economist's work to matter, policy makers must care about how they are perceived for having relied on predictions made by the economists they employ.

Moral Sentiments

Politicians, as seen here, are in the business of acquiring and retaining power. Depending on the culture in which they operate, their ability to acquire and retain power depends on their success in appealing to and maintaining the support of the voters. The sentiments of the voters are more important to politicians the more open and democratic the society. Politicians who have to stand for election care more about the sentiments of their constituents than do those who merely seize power. I will assume throughout this chapter that the "politician" in my model must get sufficient support from voters to acquire and retain power.

In *The Theory of Moral Sentiments*, Adam Smith provides a framework that we can apply to the nexus between politician and voter, so conceptualized. Smith compares what it means to "approve of" an opinion and to "adopt" that opinion. This comparison matters here because of the importance to the politician of how his stated opinions and positions affect the voter. One of the factors that govern this reality is that voters, though motivated by sentiment, believe themselves also to be motivated by facts and logic. Some voters indeed make an effort to gather the facts about the politicians who compete for their votes.

Because voters consider themselves to be rational, they recognize the difference between what is offered to them by politicians and the facts relating to those appeals. If they go to the trouble of voting at all, they must make a decision concerning which politician's opinions they choose to adopt.

Everyone has opinions, but there is a difference between how opinions matter to voters and how they matter to politicians. Because no one individual can determine who holds power, whether under a democracy or not, individual opinion is cheap. People can have whatever opinions they wish and not care about the consequences beyond how their opinions are received in their immediate social circle. They can express their opinions without substantial fear of the negative consequences of alienating those who disapprove of their opinions. Everyone is entitled to his own opinion mainly because it matters so little what that opinion is.

On the other hand, politicians must choose carefully in forming and expressing their opinions. They must *adopt* opinions with a view toward winning the *approval* of the voters to which they must appeal in order to hold power. Politicians form positions on issues with a view toward gaining the approval of the voters on whose sentiments they depend for election.

Now consider the following passage from Smith:

> To approve of another man's opinions is to adopt those opinions and to adopt those opinions is to approve of them. If the same arguments that convince you, convince me likewise, I necessarily approve of our conviction; and if they do not, I necessarily disapprove of it; neither can I possibly conceive that I should do the one without the other. To approve or disapprove, therefore, of the opinions of others is acknowledged, by everybody, to mean no more than to observe their agreement or disagreement with our own (Smith 2000, 15).

Once a politician has succeeded in getting voters to approve of his opinion, he has thereby also succeeded in getting the voters to adopt the same opinion. To approve of an opinion is to have a positive reaction to it based on sentiment. To adopt an opinion, on the other hand, is to take it upon oneself to *have* that opinion, to be convinced of the arguments in favor of it.

A second passage from *The Theory of Moral Sentiments* reads as follows:

> Every faculty in one man is the measure by which he judges of the like faculty of another. I judge of your sight by my sight, of your ear by my ear, of your reason by my reason, of your resentment by my resentment, of your love by my love. I neither have, nor can have, any other way of judging them (Smith 2000, 18).

For the economist, this means that the people to whom he gives advice judge that advice by their own standards. When their judgment is defective, it becomes the job of the economist to goad them into seeing the flaw in what they believe.

The Ladies and the Preacher

Game theorists Ken Binmore and Adam Brandenburger offer a parable about an incident that takes place during the Victorian era and that is apt here (Binmore and Brandenburger 1990). According to the parable, three Victorian ladies, Alice, Bertha, and Cora, sit down in a carriage, and—gasp!—all three have dirty faces. Each can see that the other two have dirty faces, but none knows that her own face is dirty. If any knew that her face was dirty or, more specifically, was perceived to be dirty, she would blush. But none knows and therefore none blushes. None sees the flaw in her appearance.

The ladies might well notice a snicker or two, in that each knows that each of her companions knows that there is at least one dirty face among the three present. But no one blushes—not yet anyway. Each reassures herself that she has the only clean face in the carriage. That's where things stand until a preacher enters the carriage. Then the preacher says, "At least one lady in this carriage has a dirty face."

Now everything changes. Before the preacher came along, none of the ladies could know with certainty whether her own face was dirty or not. Each lady could believe that her face is clean and believe that every other lady believes that her face is clean as well. After the preacher comes along, this is no longer true. Because of his announcement and because Victorian-era preachers are always to be believed, each lady knows that the condition of her face has become a matter of concern.

Take Alice, for example. She knows that Bertha and Cora have dirty faces but isn't sure about her own face. She then considers the possibility that her face is clean. What, then, will Bertha think? Well, Alice reasons that Bertha would consider the possibility that she, Bertha, also has a clean face, in which event both would expect Cora to blush. Why would Cora blush? Well, because neither Alice nor Bertha blushes. Even though Cora knows they have dirty faces, their refusal to blush tells her that they must see Cora as having a dirty face as well.

Now suppose that Cora doesn't blush. Then Bertha will blush because, by not blushing, Cora confirms that Bertha must have a dirty face. Then if Bertha doesn't blush, Alice will conclude that her face is dirty after all and blush.

Thus all three blush (Binmore and Brandenburger 1990, 105–106).

The importance of the parable lies in how it illustrates the difference between knowledge and common knowledge. All three ladies have dirty faces, and each lady knows that the other two have dirty faces before the preacher arrives. It takes the preacher's comment to turn the fact that all three have dirty faces into common knowledge. Now all three ladies know that all three know that all three have dirty faces (Binmore and Brandenburger 1990, 106).

If economists are to have an impact on social policy, their findings must become common knowledge. Consider the study, noted earlier, which found that the corporate tax in Germany imposed a substantial burden on workers' wages (Fuest, Peichl, and Siegloch 2015) or the CBO study that showed job losses from a $15 minimum wage (CBO 2021). It would not be enough for policy makers to know about these studies. It would be necessary also for policy makers to know that voters also know about the studies.

In order to turn their findings into common knowledge, there must be a willingness on the part of economists to unite in support of findings such as these. That does not mean blind support for the methods employed in conducting the studies but rather support for the core principle established by each (corporate taxes reduce wages, the minimum wage reduces employment), with a view toward further research aimed at improving the methods used in each. In this regard, the economist must take on the job of the preacher in the Binmore–Brandenburger parable: He must speak up in a way that makes it difficult for policy makers to ignore knowledge that their constituents have.

Cooperation and Sentiments

There has been a discussion in the economics literature about the role of cooperation in human action. Suppose people have to choose whether to cooperate on some issue. The issue might be whether to wear face masks in each other's presence, given that none has been vaccinated against COVID-19. Or it might be whether to oppose a rise in the corporate tax rate, more specifically to cooperate in ousting a politician who would raise the rate. Robert Frank has written about how "players" in a social game like this can improve the outcome of the game for themselves by building utility functions "with a conscience." He summarizes a key article as follows: "A blush may reveal a lie and cause great embarrassment at the moment. But in situations that require trust, there can be great advantage in being known to be a blusher" (Frank 1987, 593). This could occur if one of the people claims falsely to have been vaccinated or to have voted against the tax-hiking candidate. It is interesting that both Frank and Binmore–Brandenburger find the blush metaphor to be useful.

One advantage of the propensity to blush lies in the ability of people to communicate sincerity. If the other players know that I will blush if I promise to cooperate but nevertheless cheat, then he will be more likely to trust my promise to cooperate.

The Frank article spawned a lengthy debate about just how people are induced to cooperate when their short-run interests are served by noncooperation or when they are so indifferent to the lessons of economics that they won't bother to cooperate. There are in fact two debates, one about how they can be induced to cooperate and another about whether the inducement depends on a conscience that is somehow built into people's utility functions. The debate seems to center on the question whether it is appropriate to call the relevant mechanism a conscience, which was supposed to have been eliminated when the Cartesian theater was closed.

Readers schooled in economics will find it odd that I urge economists to see that taking their advice is a matter of conscience. Neoclassical economics assumes that people are rational and then proceeds from that assumption to conclusions about how people will behave under varying market conditions and government policies. It says nothing about conscience, however.

Yet, it is a matter of conscience whether to talk of corporate tax hikes as affecting only corporations and not people. Only people pay taxes. My property doesn't pay my property taxes. I do. It is likewise a matter of conscience to argue that project labor agreements save on construction costs when they don't. Project labor agreements limit bidding and thus raise construction costs. The core moral principle embedded in economic theory is that "there's no such thing as a free lunch." The economist has a moral duty to make people aware that the lunch promised by a politician isn't free at all.

As we saw, Paul Samuelson excoriated Milton Friedman for trying to "twist" the whole corpus of economics into an apology for the Chicago school and its acceptance of the assumptions that underlay the neoclassical model. Interestingly, both Samuelson and Friedman modeled the economic agent as satisfying the same rationality assumptions that behaviorists reject.

But Friedman was right about the irrelevance of economic assumptions, and Samuelson was wrong in opposing him on that point. It is time for economists of all stripes to recognize that the rationality assumption is a purely instrumental device, made to inform discussion *and* to bring about a change in the way people make economic choices. The economist might well recognize that people are irrational in important respects and still assume universal rationality in order to ply his trade. That would, in and of itself, be irrational except for the role that the analysis produced by the economist can then play in guiding or inducing people to think and act more rationally about economic issues.

Let us return to the parable with which we began this chapter. To understand the job of the economist, we can ask ourselves why the preacher would comment as he does on entering the carriage. The obvious answer would be to shame the ladies into washing their faces. Then how about the fact that once the ladies wash their faces, the preacher's comment no longer holds true? The preacher would have produced a result just the opposite of what he announced.

The preacher, we can imagine, operates on the assumption that proper ladies *should* never go out in public with dirty faces. He then produces a result that accords with this norm by creating the "common-knowledge" that every lady has a dirty face. What he takes to be the norm—no dirty faces—becomes the reality but only because of his intervention.

Suppose the preacher, before he enters the carriage, knows that there are widespread violations of the no-dirty-faces rule among Victorian ladies. He therefore knows he might be wrong to predict that every lady in the carriage would have a clean face. He might, however, tell himself that if he encounters dirty faces, he will announce the fact and thus bring about a result that renders the "no-dirty-faces" assumption valid. This is akin to what the economist can and must do in enforcing a no-irrationality norm in public policy.

Another feature of this parable that is relevant here is that, being Victorian, no lady in the carriage wishes to point out that any other lady has a dirty face. She might do this out of politeness, but she might do it also out of recognition that her own face might be dirty and that she would not want to learn that it is as a consequence of pointing out that the other ladies have a dirty face.

Thus, we have a rudimental theory of mistakes. A mistake happens if someone makes a decision that leads unintentionally to an avoidable and harmful outcome. The harm varies with the seriousness of the error. The responsibility for the harm varies with the control that the individual has over the decision. The captain of the Titanic made a mistake when he charged ahead despite warnings of ice bergs. The mistake was calamitous for most of the passengers and crew onboard, and the captain bore the full responsibility. The German people made a mistake when they gave the Nazis a parliamentary majority in 1933, with the well-known calamitous results.

What mistakes occur in the carriage before the preacher enters? They consist of the failure on the part of each lady either to point out the presence of the other dirty faces or to reach the conclusion, based on the snickering, that her own face is dirty. The consequence is the embarrassment eventually suffered when the preacher goads each toward the conclusion that her face is dirty. As embarrassing as it would have been for each lady, had her dirty face been made common knowledge before the preacher came along, it is more so after he does.

The ladies could easily have gotten the facts concerning the condition of their faces had they just spoken up or read the snickers for what they meant. But they were driven not to get the facts by the social standards of the time. They were driven by Victorian sentiment. The captain of the Titanic was driven by hubris and the German people by resentment over Versailles. They were all driven by flawed sentiments, and the flaw in their sentiments caused them to make mistakes.

The moral is that mistakes are more likely to occur the more people are driven by sentiment and poor information. The lesson for politics seems easy: Think logically rather than sentimentally. But we can't reach so simple a conclusion inasmuch as sentiment can as easily produce good outcomes as it can produce bad outcomes. The passengers on the Titanic died because of the boldness of their captain, yet the world as a whole has fared well (I would maintain, anyway) because of the boldness of Columbus. The German people fared badly under Hitler but well under Bismarck. Both leaders were militaristic. One acted out of sentiment disciplined by command of the facts. The other did not.

Thus, there is an asymmetry. Sentiments are less likely to lead to poor choices and more likely to lead to good choices the more informed they are by reason.

Before the preacher comes along, each lady in the carriage knows that the lady next to her knows that the remaining lady may believe that she has a clean face. Alice knows factually that Bertha knows factually that Cora may believe herself to have a clean face. Before the preacher comes along, this combination of facts and beliefs leads to what might be seen as a social mistake, the failure to recognize that there are dirty faces all around.

We might restate the problem as follows: Each lady has reason to ask if her face is dirty and reason to point out that the faces of the other two are dirty as well. It is sentiment—a Victorian sentiment—that stops her from doing either and thereby from settling a matter that could easily have been settled before the preacher came around.

Other economists have developed the ideas offered here in a somewhat different fashion. Samuel Fleischacker summarizes the message of Book III of Adam Smith's *Theory of Moral Sentiments* (the "deepest section" of the book) as follows:

> We judge first of others, then apply those judgments to ourselves, and it is only *because* we sometimes see ourselves as if we were one of those "others" that we are moved at all to criticize ourselves and change our behavior (Fleischacker 2004, 51).

Says Smith: "It is so disagreeable to think ill of ourselves that we often purposely turn away from those circumstances which might render judgment unfavorable" (Smith 2000, 51). The preacher-economist is needed in order to overcome the resulting "self-deceit."

Smith recognized the difficulty of getting people suffering self-deceit to see their own behavior "in an unfavorable light." Like the preacher in the carriage, the economist has to get people to see the flaw in their self-understanding indirectly. From Smith we learn that

> a would-be moral critic needs to put his criticisms of others *indirectly*, and will perhaps do best by describing their behavior in ways they can see as wrong, without putting that moral judgment in the description. If you want to point out something you think I am doing wrong, but have good reason to believe that I will hear any moral criticism as in service of my enemies, or as a reflection of your failure to understand my feelings, then you might want to avoid any directly moral comment on my behavior and try to arouse my moral judgment against my own actions, by way of simply describing the effects of my actions on my victims, in dry but imaginative detail (Smith 2000, 51–52).

Thus, in the carriage, the preacher does not embarrass the ladies by simply saying, "You all have dirty faces." Rather he suggests that at least one lady is making the other two uncomfortable over her dirty face. If a politician wants to raise the corporate tax rate in the name of "equity," the economist should not argue, as he might, that equity is an entirely subjective goal, devoid of any scientific basis. Rather, he should argue that it does not serve equity to enact a tax change that depresses wages.

What Economists Can't Do

Thus, economists can't further their aims by attacking the core values of noneconomists who are driven by sentiment. They need to make their point "indirectly." Economists can warn politicians (or fellow economists) against making promises that they would not be willing to see tested in any rigorous manner. I have suggested that the promises of politicians could be tested in a manner that would improve the quality of the decisions they make. The core task facing the economist-preacher is similar to the one facing the preacher in the carriage, who got his lady companions to recognize that they had dirty faces by stating simply that there was at least one dirty face in the carriage.

Economists cannot change policy without changing the political culture that ignores the importance of accountability in offering and taking economic advice. Furthermore, economists can't change the political culture until they determine how, in addressing policy, they make politicians and therefore themselves more accountable to an electorate that is driven mainly by sentiment.

It is possible, fortunately, to increase accountability when it comes to economic policy. In the section that follows, I will outline five paths to accountability: (1) tests of the accuracy of predictions, (2) cost–benefit tests, (3) general equilibrium modeling of proposed policy changes, (4) identification of policy changes that make accountability easier to achieve, and (5) critical examination of constraints that are imposed on market choices and that undermine accountability.

These methods are aimed at the core objective, which is to get voters driven by sentiment to demand increased accountability from politicians driven by a wish to hold and exercise power. Like everyone else, politicians would prefer to win and hold office without having to be held accountable. They enlist economists in their efforts to dodge accountability. Those economists then become part of the problem. I want to outline a procedure whereby economists who wish to increase account-ability—and who are willing themselves to be held accountable—can ply their trade.

What Economists Can Do

The parable about the ladies in the carriage is predicated on a cultural expectation of accountability. The ladies are accountable to the standards of their time. There is a lapse in their attentiveness to those standards, which becomes the job of the preacher to correct.

The one bedrock standard of advanced democratic societies is that voters, though they act on the basis of sentiment, do not wish to be seen as irrational. Nor can politicians openly treat voters as irrational without alienating them.

One goal of the economist is to compel the politician to concede that his opinions or the position he takes on some issue is predicated on senti-ment rather than fact. The economist does voters a service when he is able to isolate the facts and separate them from the sentiments that are behind the politician's appeal for their approval.

It is on this principle that the economist must predicate his work. Consumers expect accountability from their car dealers, and voters can be induced to expect it from their elected leaders. The economist begins his work here by getting voters to understand how readily they allow them-selves to be taken in by politicians.

The task in this section is to outline a role for economists in reversing this process. The method available to economists is to challenge politi-cians simply to identify the means by which they have chosen to hold themselves accountable. If a politician promises that he can raise the cor-porate tax rate without hurting workers, he should be prepared to defend that promise if he does raise the corporate tax rate.

The voter may or may not adopt the opinions or positions of a candi-date for office and may or may not bother to vote at all, with little to fear in terms of the personal consequences, whatever the opinions adopted and whatever the choice to vote or not. Yet, voters do think about the issues and do, by definition, vote. Thus, it is realistic to imagine that they would be open to the available methods for demanding accountability.

One such method consists of a test of the accuracy of a prediction. Consider again a proposal to impose a minimum wage law. The proponents of the minimum wage promise that there will be no harmful effects to labor. A statistical test would consist of the construction and estimation of a model that would separate the effects on jobs and employment from the effects that resulted from other factors.

It might be argued that a test of this kind would be inconclusive because of factors (e.g., a slowing economy) other than the minimum wage that would affect employment. Consider two policy lines for which theory and evidence are quite mixed concerning their economic effects—minimum wage laws and foreign trade policy. Any attempt to achieve accountability in the instance of imposing a minimum wage law or adopting a restrictive trade policy may be doomed to frustration just because the effects of both are so hard to sort out. There are, however, policies other than minimum wage laws or trade restrictions for which accountability is easier to achieve and that are arguably more defensible on ethical grounds. The thoughtful voter might, for example, ask whether there were alternative ways of achieving the intended effects of the minimum wage that were also more transparent for their economic effects.

Both minimum wage laws and trade restrictions are ham-fisted ways of helping low-income people. An increase in the earned income tax credit is, arguably, ethically superior because it provides an improved safety net for nonworking poor people as well as working poor people.

The task of sorting out the effects on labor of the earned income tax credit is far easier than the task of sorting out the effects of a minimum wage or tariff. The economist should point this out to voters in his efforts to get them to demand more accountability.

A second method consists of subjecting the proposed policy to a cost–benefit test, as for example, the cost–benefit test of the Cape Wind project discussed earlier. This approach is particularly suitable for public projects funded by tax revenues or for private projects subsidized out of tax revenues.

A cost–benefit test induces persons on both sides of an issue to own up to the costs and benefits they impute to the project. If the proponent of a "wind farm," for example, has to claim unrealistically high benefits in order to rationalize a project on cost–benefit terms, then he implicitly admits the weakness of his position.

Next, it is possible to assess certain policies, particularly trade and tax policies, by building a computable general equilibrium or "CGE" model of the economy and then using the model to see how the proposed policy affects the economy as represented by the model. Economists can increase accountability by encouraging voters and politicians to "think inside the box"—to utilize the framework provided by a computer model to prod politicians into owning up to the assumptions they make about the economic effects of proposed policy changes.

Both this approach and the cost–benefit approach instill discipline and accountability into the political process by requiring parties on both sides of the issue, whatever it might be, to state explicitly how they would measure costs and benefits or how they would specify the general equilibrium model being used.

This includes finding out what the evidence shows—of choosing the elasticities with which to parameterize the model. How would a higher corporate tax rate affect investment? How would the minimum wage affect employment? Again, this is not to make assumptions about how people would in fact choose, given that they are not, in fact, rational. Rather, it is to make assumptions about how they would choose, were they rational, rationality in public choice being the principal duty of the economist to encourage.

Finally, the economist should make the voter wary of the constraints that politicians impose on private sector choices, if only because of the possibility that, in imposing these constraints, they are making accountability less attainable. The Gulf oil spill of 2010 resulted in part because constraints on drilling under less risky circumstances pushed the oil companies into drilling in deep waters. It turns out that the models that the Minerals and Management Service required the oil companies to use in assessing the risks of drilling in these waters were flawed and thus failed to identify the high probability of an oil spill.

Someone should have raised a red flag when Congress voted against drilling in safer areas without due attention to the risks of pushing oil drilling in deep waters. The general principle is that constraints imposed on market activities require the creation of mechanisms for evaluating the economic consequences of those constraints.

There is an important difference between economics as a predictive science (or art) and economics as an instrument for societal change. "Unrealistic" assumptions are a useful instrument for predicting the effects of a tax on cigarettes. But unrealistic assumptions are a useful instrument also for changing the way people think about economic issues insofar as they induce people to think rationally about those issues and, in doing so, to vindicate the assumptions.

In this context, it is important to remember that the subject of the economist's inquiry is a cognitive actor with the capacity, but not necessarily the inclination, to think rationally about issues. In this context, the economist cannot be agnostic about his assumptions since the usefulness of his models depends on how people respond to policies he analyzes. In this sense, the job of the economist is to foster rational choice by making assumptions about individual behavior that are demonstrably wrong but that will prove fruitful for making accurate predictions.

Economists now recognize that preferences are endogenous. It is time for them to recognize also that rationality is endogenous. One may, if one wishes, adopt the libertarian idea that people should be permitted to choose and act as they please provided that they harm no one else. The problem for the policy advisor, however, is that government policies affect the constraints under which people make private choices and therefore affect the incentives that people have to choose rationally. Then also government can institute programs that have the purpose and the effect of rescuing people from the consequences of irrational choices made in part because government, in effect, helped create conditions that encouraged those choices.

This brings to mind the problem of moral hazard, which arises from the problem of insuring the individual against risks that he can avoid only by exercising his own personal care. Insurance companies write deductibles into their policies to shift the risk of minor accidents from themselves to their customers. Rational policy making aims at shifting responsibility for personal decisions from government to the individual.

The difference between the problem of endogenous rationality and moral hazard is that there is nothing inherently irrational on the part of the individual who adopts risky behavior when someone is willing to insure him against the consequences of that behavior. If I know that the insurance company will pay for my broken taillight when I back my car out of a parking space, my diminished willingness to take due care is rational. Endogenous rationality, as discussed here, is more akin to the decision by a teenager with a newly acquired driver's license to drag race in his father's Corvette. Every father knows that forestalling such behavior is necessary because the teen who would engage in it is not choosing rationally.

In earlier chapters, I noted how other economists have criticized the neoclassical model for, in effect, dehumanizing the economic actor, by reducing the decision maker to a system of preferences. Proponents of these schools of thought argue that, contrary to the assumptions of neoclassical economics, actual persons choose inconsistently and exhibit other patterns of behavior that the neoclassical assumptions exclude.

John B. Davis, for example, points out that the neoclassical model requires transitivity of choice. Thus, in his words, the need for this assumption "trumps empirical considerations. This kind of practice, of course, is what psychologists and behavioral economists, who have made a careful empirical investigation of economic choice behavior, find so disturbing about rational choice theory" (Davis 2003, 43).

At the risk of further disturbing the same psychologists and behavioral economists, let's suppose, for example, that three budget policies, A, B, and C, are put before the electorate. The policies call, in order, for high taxes and spending, moderate taxes and spending, and low taxes and spending. Suppose that today voter Alice prefers A to B to C but tomorrow prefers C to A to B. Davis' complaint is that the voter is assumed to prefer A to C today even though in fact she prefers C to A just a day later.

In fact, however, Alice's inconsistent behavior is one reason why the economist should assume that she is consistent. If the economist is speaking to Alice today, he is speaking to her when she prefers A to C. He cannot and should not attempt to second-guess her preferences tomorrow. What he can do is confront Alice with the fact that if she prefers A to B and B to C today, she must prefer A to C today in order to choose rationally. Then if Alice considers reversing her preference between A and C tomorrow, she is compelled to see that reversal for what it is—a change in what she previously saw to be rational. Thus, the economist performs the service of getting Alice to understand that in order for her choices *not* to be inconsistent, she must have the information she needs in order to choose consistently.

In the Ricardian example of Chapter 2, the economist does not begin by assuming that the individual thinks rationally. He begins by noting some issue about which the individual thinks, for example, about whether real or opportunity costs should determine trade flows. If that issue has to do with the provision of wine to British consumers and if it requires the economist to goad people into thinking about opportunity costs, rather than real costs, then that is what the economist must do. In thus goading them to think differently, the economist is recognizing that their willingness to think rationality is endogenous to his efforts.

In *On Adam Smith's Wealth of Nations*, Fleischacker writes at length about Smith's insistence on the importance of education to "freedom" as well as to "the ordinary duties of private life" (Fleischacker 2004, 235). Fleischacker interprets Smith as arguing that "fostering rationality and the capacity for judgment is therefore a way of *restoring* liberty" to people (Fleischacker 2004, 235).

Certainly then Smith was trying to foster rationality, albeit through education. The argument here is that education will not suffice and, indeed, can lead people toward less rational choices depending on exactly what it is that they are taught. Fleischacker quotes commentator David Marshall as saying that "Smith understands both our relation to others and our relation to ourselves in a thoroughly theatrical way: We are 'constantly imagining ourselves appearing before the eyes of other people'" (Fleischacker 2004, 13). In a similar fashion, another commentator, Charles Griswold, sees Smith as meaning "that we constantly adopt one or another type of mask, and thereby distance ourselves both from ourselves and from other people" (Fleischacker 2004, 13).

Fleischacker goes on to say that

> to the extent that Smith engages in political persuasion, uses a dialogic style or represses dialogue with a monologic voice, or employs dramatic and other forms from fictional literature to illustrate or structure his writing on political economy, we need to read him more carefully than we might read Milton Friedman or Kenneth Arrow (Fleischacker 2004, 14).

I would argue that, Smith's style through the *Wealth of Nations* and especially through the *Theory of Moral Sentiments* is as much aimed at persuading as it is at informing. And his method of persuasion is eclectic, drawing on various rhetorical devices in order to make his point. Fleischacker enumerates words used by Smith to describe the objects of his scorn—"follies," "delusions," "prejudices" among them. For Smith,

> Absurdities and follies are not just falsehoods but falsehoods so glaring that, once they are pointed out, no reasonable person can go on believing them. Delusions are diseased perceptions, fancies or fantasies that ought simply to vanish if one's senses can be cured (Fleischacker 2004, 24).

Thus, the economist cannot merely preach. He must goad his audience into abandoning follies and delusions.

As mentioned, authors Richard H. Thaler and Cass R. Sustein have used the word "nudge" rather than "goad," to describe what I mean here. Their term reflects the idea that they favor a kind of "libertarian paternalism" that recognizes the ultimate sovereignty of the individual in making informed choices. I prefer the stronger term.

Individual voters need to be goaded, rather than just nudged. The premise of the book *Nudge* is that people suffer from overconfidence, status quo bias, framing and other biases that cause them to make bad choices, creating an argument for government to nudge them toward making better choices. Their argument is good as far as it goes, but it makes the mistake of presupposing a government aimed somehow at promoting individual well-being rather than a government that enjoys wielding power for its own sake.

Thus, Thaler and Sunstein make the very enlightened suggestion that patients be permitted to opt out of the right to sue doctors for malpractice as a way of reducing health care costs. What they miss, however, is that the plaintiffs' bar would claim that a patient would be too overconfident about his doctor to be trusted with the right to opt out of the right to sue.

The more fundamental obstacle to progress of the kind hoped for by Thaler and Sunstein is the fact that government has a vested interest in getting people to make bad choices. The authors themselves devote an entire chapter to showing how Sweden failed to apply the appropriate "nudge" in privatizing social security (though they cite other examples, in which government did nudge appropriately).

Economists qua preachers cannot therefore merely "nudge." Because voters think and act out of flawed sentiment, it is necessary to *goad* them into rethinking the policy positions that their elected leaders have adopted. That's a job for a preacher, not a libertarian.

The economist thus tries to get the individual to rethink his optimization calculus in such a way as to bring about optimum results. In this context, it is not that the economist who has a means–ends problem to solve, but that the individual is in need of having the appropriate means–ends problem presented to him for solution. Thaler and Sunstein describe this as the need to present a suitable "choice architecture" for making private choices. The difference is that voters need a similar choice architecture in choosing how to respond to the policy positions offered to them by the very politicians who would do the "nudging."

The economist recasts the means–ends problem confronting the individual economic agent so that it can be solved rationally rather than irrationally. This brings to mind the arguments from cognitive science to the effect that people are conflicted actors whose decisions are more a matter of chance than of purposeful action. There may be several agents or "homonuclei" at war within the person, all competing to cause him to choose one action or another. Choices emerge out of the individual's thinking, but there is no captain at the helm in his brain, or so say the cognitive scientists. The individual acts but not for reasons he can necessarily articulate. The individual thinks that he chooses rationally but does in fact choose rationally only under properly constrained conditions.

The economist does not have to take responsibility for whatever inconsistencies plague the thought process of the person who seeks (or, at least, needs) his advice. It doesn't matter if the person learned to appreciate classical music and vintage wine over his lifetime or just recently developed a taste for rap or heroin. It is the decision maker, warts and all, who presents himself for examination and whose tastes are what they are at that moment.

In that context, the economist has a duty to develop a framework based on rational choice. In proceeding in this fashion, he cannot hope to change policy directly by appealing directly to logic. He can hope only to change minds by causing politicians to see that others believe them to have been thinking and choosing irrationally.

Because economists do not have mirrors to hold up to people's thought processes, they can influence those processes only indirectly and only through psychology. An economist can get politicians to think rationally about a minimum wage but not by showing them that their thinking is based on flawed logic. He can get them to think rationally by showing that voters believe that their thinking is based on flawed logic. The economist must therefore take on the role of the preacher in the carriage who causes the others around him to see that they are not seen as they would wish. The job of the economist is to manipulate perceptions to the end of bringing about a more rational social order, not to take the existing social order as a given and immutable to change. His job is to goad, not just nudge.

References

Aquinas, S.T. 1950. "Summa Theologica." In *Early Economic Thought*, ed. A.E. Monroe. Cambridge, MA: Harvard University Press.

Aristotle. 1951. "The Politics." In *Early Economic Thought*, ed. A.E. Monroe, pp. 3–29. Cambridge, MA: Harvard University Press.

Binmore, K., and A. Brandenburger. 1990. "Common Knowledge and Game Theory." In *Essays on the Foundations of Game Theory*, 105–150. Cambridge, Massachusetts: Basil Blackwell.

Boettke, P.J. 1999. *Socialism and the Market: the Socialist Calculation Debate Revisited*, 7. Psychology Press.

Buchanan, J.M. 1964. "What Should Economists Do?" *Southern Economic Journal*, pp. 213–222.

Caplan, B. 2007. *The Myth of the Rational Voter*. Princeton, NJ: Princeton University Press.

CBO 2021. *The Budgetary Effects of the Raise the Wage Act of 2021*. Washington DC.

Chiou, L., and E. Muehlegger. 2014. "Consumer Response to Cigarette Excise Tax Changes." *National Tax Journal* 67, no. 3, pp. 621–650.

Churchland, P.M. 1981. "Eliminative Materialism and the Propositional Attitudes." *The Journal of Philosophy* 78, no. 2, pp. 67–90.

Clark, A. 1998. *Being There*. Cambridge, Massahusetts: MIT Press.

Cowan, T. 1993. "The Scope and Limits of Preference Sovereignty." *Economics & Philosophy* 9, no. 2, pp. 253–269.

Davis, J.B. 2003. *The Theory of the Individual in Economics: Identity and Value*. New York, NY: Routledge.

Dennett, D.C. 1989. *The Intentional Stance*. Cambridge, MA: MIT Press.

Dennett, D.C. 1991. *Consciousness Explained*. Boston, MA: Little, Brown and Company.

Fleischacker, S. 2004. *On Adam Smith's Wealth of Nations*. Princeton, NJ: Princeton University Press.

Frank, R.H. 1987. If Homo Economicus Could Choose His Own Utility Function, Would He Want One with a Conscience? *American Economic Review* 77, no. 4, pp. 593–604.

Freedman, C.F. 2008. *Chicago Fundamentalism: Ideology and Methodology in Economics*. Singapore: World Scientific Publishing Co. Pte. Ltd.

Friedman, M. 2008. *The Methodology of Positive Economics*. Cambridge, UK: Cambridge University Press.

Fuest, C., A. Peichl, and S. Siegloch. 2015. "Do Higher Corporate Taxes Reduce Wages?"

Glimcher, P.W. 2011. *Foundations of Neuroeconomic Analysis*. Oxford, UK: Oxford University Press.

Haughton, J., D. Giuffre, J. Barrett, and D.G. Tuerck. 2004. *An Economic Analysis of a Wind Farm in Nantucket Sound*. Beacon Hill Institute at Suffolk University, Boston, MA.

Hayek, F.A. 1976. *The Sensory Order*. Chicago, IL: University of Chicago Press.

Holz-Eakin, D., and M. Mandel. 2015. *Dynamic Scoring and Infrastructure Spending*. Retrieved from New York, NY.

Jevons, W.S. 1879. *The Theory of Political Economy*. Macmillan and Company.

Kahneman, D. 2011. *Thinking Fast and Slow*. New York, NY: Farrar, Straus and Giroux.

Keane, M.P. 2011. "Labor Supply and Taxes: A Survey." *Journal of Economic Literature* 49, no. 4, pp. 961–1075.

Kelton, S. 2020. *The Deficit Myth: Modern Monetary Theory and the Birth of the People's Economy*. New York, NY: Public Affairs.

Keynes, J.M. 1936. *The General Theory of Employment, Interest, and Money*. London: Macmillan.

Knight, F. 1921. *Risk, Uncertainty & Profit*. New York, NY: Harper & Row, Publishers.

Lewis, M. 2017. *The Undoing Project: A Friendship That Changed Our Minds*. New York, NY: W. W. Norton & Company.

Mises, L. V. 1949. *Human Action*. Chicago, Illinois: Contemporary Books.

Muller, J.Z. 2002. "Edmund Burke: Commerce, Conservatism, and the Intellectuals." In *The Mind and the Market: Capitalism in Western Thought*, 104–138. New York, NY: Anchor Press.

Muller, J.Z. 2002. "Justus Moser: The Market as a Destroyer of Culture." In *The Mind and the Market: Capitalism in Western Thought*, 84–103. New York, NY: Anchor Books.

Muller, J.Z. 2002. "Voltaire: A Merchant of a Noble Kind." In *The Mind and the Market: Capitalism in Western Thought*, 20–50. New York, NY: Anchor Books.

Mulligan, C.B. 2012. *The Redistribution Recessiion: How Labor Market Distortions Contracted the Economy*. Oxford: Oxford University Press.

Neuroeconomics: Decision Making and the Brain. 2009. P.W. Glimcher, C.F. Camerer, E.Fehr, and R.A. Pollack eds. London, UK: Academic Press.

Ricardo, D. 1911. *Principles of Political Economy and Taxation*. E.P. Dutton & Co., Inc.

Robbins, L. 1932. *An Essay on the Nature and Significance of Economic Science*. New York, NY: St. Martin's Press.

Ross, D. 2005a. *Economic Theory and Cognitive Science: Micro Explanation*. Cambridge, MA: MIT Press.

Ross, D. 2005b. *Economic Theory and Cognitive Science: Micro Explanation*. Cambridge, MA: MIT Press.

Ross, D., and P. Dumouchel. 2004. "Emotions as Strategic Signals." *Rationality and Society* 16, no. 3, pp. 251–286.

Rothschild, E. 2001. *Economic Sentiments: Adam Smith, Condorcet, and the Enlightenment*. Cambridge, MA: Harvard University Press.

Rubin, P. H. 2003. Folk Economics. *Southern Economic Journal* 70, no. 1, pp. 157–171.

Samuelson, P.A. 1963. "Discussion." *American Economic Review* 53, no. 2, pp. 231–236.

Satz, D., and J. Ferejohn. 1994. "Rational Choice and Social Theory." *The Journal of Philosophy* 91,no. 2, pp. 71–87.

Searle, J.R. 2004. *Mind: A Brief Introduction*. New York, NY: Oxford University Press.

Sen, A.K. 1977. "Rational Fools: A Critique of the Behavioral Foundations of Economic Theory." *Philosophy & Public Affairs*, pp. 317–344.

Shermer, M. 2008. *The Mind of the Market*. New York, NY: Henry Holt and Company.

Smith, A. 1976a. *An Inquiry into the Natue and Causes of The Wealth of Nations*, 1. Chicago Illinois: The University of Chicago Press.

Smith, A. 1976b. *An Inquiry into the Nature and Causes of the Wealth of Nations*, 2. Chicago, IL: University of Chicago Press.

Smith, A. 1982. "History of Astronomy." In *Essays on Philosophical Subjects,* ed. W.P.D. Wightman. Liberty Fund, Inc.

Smith, A. 2000. *The Theory of Moral Sentiments*. Amherst, New York, NY: Prometheous Books.

Soto, J.H.D. 2008. *The Austrian School: Market Order and Entreneurial Creativity*. Cheltenham, UK: Edward Elgar.

Stigler, G.J. 1982. *The Economist as Preacher and Other Essays*. Chicago, IL: University of Chicago Press.

Stringham, E.P. 2010. "Economic Value and Costs are Subjective." In *Handbook on Contemporary Austrian Economics*, ed. P.J. Boetke. Cheltenham, UK: Edward Elger.

Stringham, E.P. 2011. *Anarchy and the Law: the Political Economy of Choice*, 1. Transaction Publishers.

Tawney, R.H. 2015. *Religion and the Rise of Cpitalism: A Historical Study*. New York, NY: Verso.

Thaler, R.H., and C.R. Sunstein. 2008. *Nudge: Improving Decisions About Health, Wealth, and Happiness*. New Haven, CT: Yale University Press.

Tuerck, D.G. 2010. "Why Project Labor Agreements are Not in the Public Interest." *Cato Journal* 301, pp. 45–64.

Tuerck, D.G. 2021. *Macroeconomics*, 3rd ed. New York, NY: Business Expert Press.

Turing, A.M. 1950. *Computing Machinery and Intelligence.* Oxford: Oxford University Press.

Tversky, A., and D. Kahneman. 1981. "The Framing of Decisions and the Psychology of Choice." *Science* 211, no. 4481, pp. 453–458.

Wittman, D. 1995. *The Myth of Democratic Failure.* Chicago: University of Chicago Press.

About the Author

David G. Tuerck is President of the Beacon Hill Institute, a Massachusetts economic research organization that specializes in modeling tax law changes. He is also Professor Emeritus at Suffolk University in Boston, where he served on the economics faculty for 38 years. He received his PhD in economics from the University of Virginia. Before joining Suffolk, he worked as a director in the economic consulting practice at Coopers & Lybrand in Washington, DC. During his tenure at Coopers & Lybrand, he served as a consultant to the U.S. Treasury on modeling the Reagan tax policy proposals. He has published in the academic literature and testified before Congress and state legislatures on numerous occasions and on a number of public policy issues.

Index

www.ingramcontent.com/pod-product-compliance
Lightning Source LLC
Chambersburg PA
CBHW061326220326
41599CB00026B/5061